Coming of Age

Coming of Age

A Treasury of Poems, Quotations and Readings to Celebrate Growing Up

COLLECTED BY EDWARD SEARL

Skinner House Books
Boston

Copyright © 2007 by Edward Searl. Published by Skinner House Books, an imprint of the Unitarian Universalist Association of Congregations, a liberal religious organization with more than 1,000 congregations in the United States and Canada. 25 Beacon St., Boston, MA 02108. All rights reserved.

ISBN 978-1-55896-512-6

Printed in the United States

Cover art *Winged Companion*, © 2002 Eleanor Rubin, http://ellyrubinjournal. typepad.com

16 15 14 13
6 5 4 3 2

We gratefully acknowledge permission to reprint copyrighted materials starting on page 161.

Library of Congress Cataloging-in-Publication Data

Searl, Edward, 1947-
  Coming of age : a treasury of poems, quotations, and readings on growing up / collected by Edward Searl.
      p. cm.
  Includes index.
  ISBN-13: 978-1-55896-512-6 (pbk. : alk. paper)
  ISBN-10: 1-55896-512-2 (pbk. : alk. paper) 1. Spiritual life—Unitarian Universalist churches. 2. Youth—Religious life. 3. Teenagers—Religious life. I. Title.

BX9855.S43 2007
808.8'0354—dc22

2006025469

Contents

Dear Reader,

A typical life has four major transitions. Birth and death, of course, frame a life span. Both happen at a precise moment. And like them, marriage happens all at once, often in the midst of our culture's most elaborate ritual. But coming of age, the mysterious passage from childhood into adulthood, is fundamentally different. The transition is a long journey, often spanning a decade. There are various cultural markers, such as entering high school, acquiring a driver's license, or turning twenty-one, but at heart becoming a grown-up is a private journey. Each adolescent achieves maturity in fits and starts. There is no single defining observance.

Over time, the unfolding life experiences of adolescence take on a mythic quality. Adults who love someone this age often remember the intensity and poignancy of their own teenage years. These experiences and memories inspire us to express the wonderful tumult of growing up with frank and loving words.

The poems, quotations, and readings of this collection chronicle the physical, behavioral, and emotional changes of adolescence, as well as the exciting potential of this age. Whether you are watching over the growth of someone you love or arching toward adulthood yourself, I hope that the words offered here will help you better understand the challenges and triumphs of becoming one's essential self.

In affirmation and expectation,

Edward Searl

The Soul Unfolds

On Self-Knowledge

And a man said, "Speak to us of Self-Knowledge."

And he answered, saying:

Your hearts know in silence the secrets of the days and the nights.

But your ears thirst for the sound of your heart's knowledge.

You would know in words that which you have always known in thought.

You would touch with your fingers the naked body of your dreams.

And it is well you should.

The hidden well-spring of your soul must needs rise and run murmuring to the sea;

And the treasure of your infinite depths would be revealed to your eyes.

But let there be no scales to weigh your unknown treasure;

And seek not the depths of your knowledge with staff or sounding line.

For self is a sea boundless and measureless.

Say not, "I have found the truth," but rather, "I have found a truth."

Say not, "I have found the path of the soul." Say rather, "I have met the soul walking upon my path."

For the soul walks upon all paths.

The soul walks not upon a line, neither does it grow like a reed.

The soul unfolds itself, like a lotus of countless petals.

KAHLIL GIBRAN

We do not grow absolutely, chronologically. We grow sometimes in one dimension, and not in another, unevenly. We grow partially. We are relative. We are mature in one realm, childish in another. The past, present, and future mingle and pull us backward, forward, or fix us in the present. We are made up of layers, cells, constellations.

ANAÏS NIN

"It's time to light the candles to the mothers and grandmothers," I said. Just saying these words seemed to drive the night's chill from my bones.

Melynda was silent, but her eyes never left mine. We removed the candles from our sack and separated the wicks. I opened the nylon doorway of the tent and felt a surprising gust of night wind. The stars were poised and waiting. Melynda and I crouched, leaned out the green door flap with our upper bodies, and set to work.

First, I made a small circle in the earth with our only spoon. Next we made four holes for our candles around the circle. We put candles in the holes and secured them by packing dirt up on the sides.

"Let's light them," said Melynda, her face glowing in the moonlight. I grabbed the lighter.

"I light this candle to invite the spirit and strength of my mother to help guide this young woman as she comes of age, that she will grow wise, strong, and compassionate."

The candle flickered in the breeze. Melynda cupped her hands around it for protection. I moved my hand to the second candle.

"I light this candle to invite the spirit and strength of the grandmothers to help guide this young woman as she comes of age, that she will grow wise, strong, and compassionate. Let her know on this night the secrets of womanhood so that her knowledge of herself will guide her on life's difficult journey."

Again, the candle flickered. The boars moaned in the distant rocks. I was now ready to light the third candle.

"I light this candle to invite the spirit of our community of women, the teachers, the neighbors, the friends. Let their strength and wisdom guide and protect her as she comes of age so that she will know that there are many whose strength she can rely on when the road becomes difficult and her limbs grow weary."

The flames cast dancing shadows on the circle while brightening the entryway to our tent. The sky and stars felt inexplicably closer, more protective than distant, more kin than foe. I lit the final candle.

"I light this candle to invite the spirit of this mother and daughter to let their strength and wisdom be known to each other. I light this candle in a spirit of hope that their relationship will grow and deepen with the years. May they learn from each other and respect each other now and throughout all the changes of their lives. Let all the spirits come!"

Melynda and I cradled our hands together in a protective circle around the four candles. The wind beat against the backs of our hands, but we were able to protect the flames for a minute more: four kitchen candles burning outside a cheap dome-tent, a mother and adolescent daughter reaching out to protect the flames they have lit together. We nodded to each other and blew out the candles, our eyes wide and our cheeks flushed with excitement. We removed the candles from the soil, packed them away, and zipped ourselves back into the tent. Our hands were stiff from being exposed to the night air and a chill ran through us both.

"Now what?" Melynda asked.

"Now, we talk, all night if you like. Now, you ask me any questions in your head about me, about your body, about my relationship with your father, about my mother. . . . Anything."

"Anything?" she said, looking up, dead serious.

"Anything," I responded, without fear.

We talked till the morning light started to warm the tent walls. She asked me questions and I answered with an open heart, using the best words I could. We talked about her body, mine, my mother's, the rough words she had heard her father and me speak years before, her fears about them, the truth, the truth without fear, without disguise. Melynda spoke of her life as well, of being a girl in middle school, the pressures, fears, and desires. I listened to everything she said without flinching, somehow strengthened by the space we had created and by the spirits of the ancestral women we had invoked. We talked until there was no more to say or to ask and we fell asleep, clinging to each other with a newfound innocence, knowledge, and shared strength.

MARYANN WOODS-MURPHY

One of the signs of passing youth is the birth of a sense of fellowship with other human beings as we take our place among them.

Virginia Woolf

Maturity involves being honest and true to oneself, making decisions based on a conscious internal process, assuming responsibility for one's decisions, having healthy relationships with others and developing one's own true gifts. It involves thinking about one's environment and deciding what one will and won't accept.

Mary Pipher

Sigmund Freud was once asked to describe the characteristics of maturity, and he replied: *lieben un arbeiten* ("loving and working"). The mature adult is one who can love and allow himself or herself to be loved and who can work productively, meaningfully, and with satisfaction.

David Elkind

Instruction

The coach has taught her how to swing,
run bases, slide, how to throw
to second, flip off her mask for fouls.

Now, on her own, she studies
how to knock the dirt out of her cleats,
hitch up her pants, miss her shoulder
with a stream of spit, bump
her fist into her catcher's mitt,
and stare incredulously at the ump.

CONRAD HILBERRY

I think we all have been looking at our youth a little differently,
knowing that a most powerful alchemy—a promising, perishable,
volatile, exalted, and delicate alchemy—is occurring within them. This
alchemy is the process of discerning and becoming who they will be
beyond the families of their birth, as adults in the larger world. This
process, of course, is unending and continual. One has to be dead for
this process to be finished. We are all still trying to figure out what it
means to be a human being, what it means to be an adult. In adolescence, nonetheless, this process is especially formative and formidable.

JOHN GIBBONS

Think when you were twelve or thirteen or fourteen or fifteen and which events seemed to lurch you toward adulthood, and by necessity, then away from childhood. For me, one such event involved an apple pie.

On a typical October day—one which I now remember as stunningly blue and crisp and clear—my family was preparing to go camping. My mother had begun to make an apple pie to take with us when our friend and neighbor came into the kitchen, hysterical. She had just received word that her son had died in a car accident at college. She needed my father to call the college to find out if this were true.

As an adult, thirty years later, I still haven't come to terms with that afternoon. And at the time, as a twelve-year-old my first reaction was that of any child—to run. But how does one escape such tragedy and sorrow?

I sat on my bed, as the blue sky darkened, watching as friends and relatives made their way, shoulders slumped, to our neighbor's home. I finally went downstairs, realizing I must do what I could. But what does one do, especially when one is twelve?

The scraps of pie crust dough lay scattered over the counter; the neglected apple slices were beginning to brown a bit. I scattered the slices densely in the crust, dotted them with butter—lots of butter—and sprinkled the mixture with an abundance of cinnamon and sugar; and I carefully covered it all with the second layer of crust.

Of course I didn't realize it at the time, but in putting together that pie, I was making the effort to join the world of adults, to take responsibility and to take care and, most importantly, to come to terms with an unavoidable sorrow. I may not have fallen headlong into adulthood that afternoon, but I was stumbling my way there.

And I think that's what most of us do: stumble our way toward adulthood.

SUSAN MORRISON HEBBLE

Adolescence has been recognised as a stage of human development since medieval times—long, long before the industrial revolution—and, as it is now, has long been seen as a phase which centers on the fusion of sexual and social maturity. Indeed, adolescence as a concept has as long a history as that of puberty, which is sometimes considered more concrete, and hence much easier to name and to recognise.

TERRI APTER

It's not that I really needed to know about condoms and sex, and my father probably knew that. But I did need for my father to say, in his own way, "I see and affirm that you have become a man." And I wonder when his father did that for him and wonder if I have done that for my sons, as well.

This is the ritual dance between parents and children. We are always both ahead of and way behind one another in our rites of passage. Everything we do in our growing up has been done before. But it needs recognition and validation each time for each one of us—public, private, and secret. *The rituals must be observed.* The rituals are cairns marking the path behind us and ahead of us. Without them we lose our way.

ROBERT FULGHUM

With the establishment of a good relationship to the world of skills and tools, and with the advent of sexual maturity, childhood proper comes to an end. Youth begins. But in puberty and adolescence all samenesses and continuities relied on earlier are questioned again, because of a rapidity of body growth which equals that of early childhood and because of the entirely new addition of physical genital maturity. The growing and developing youths, faced with this physiological revolution within them, are now primarily concerned with what they appear to be in the eyes of others as compared with what they feel they are, and with the question of how to connect the roles and skills cultivated earlier with the occupational prototypes of the day. In their search for a new sense of continuity and sameness, adolescents have to refight many of the battles of earlier years, even though to do so they must artificially appoint perfectly well-meaning people to play the roles of enemies; and they are ever ready to install lasting idols and ideals as guardians of final identity.

ERIK H. ERIKSON

In "premodern" or "simple" societies, a huge amount of resources is poured into making the transition clear and unmistakable and ensuring that the entrance into adult society is successful and timely. In modern society, the transition is often drawn out, the signs and symbols of it subtle, and the period of adolescence extended.

In our culture, there are few clear and powerful rites of passage that help adolescents to make meaning of their status and to become adults. The meaning of "adulthood" is often left for the individual to define. Are you an adult when you graduate from high school? When you are eligible for the draft and can vote? When you are of legal drinking age?

Are you an adult when you begin to work full time? When you move out on your own? When you are no longer financially dependent on your parents? The boundaries that mark adulthood in our society are not clear, nor are they agreed upon. The transition into adulthood is not imbued with so much meaning as to make it understood by those who undergo it or by the culture as a whole.

WENDY L. BELL

In the 1960s, the term *identity crisis* was used loosely to describe the volatile nature of the teenage years. Yet, rather than describing a troubling quality, the term actually refers to a teenager's developmental struggle with the question: *Who am I?*

During this time of self-scrutiny, the teen needs to look inward, to consider personal history, and gain perspective on past, present, and future. Exploration will give way to reorganization into a cohesive sense of self that satisfies both internal needs and external demands. The resulting sense of self will encompass an autonomous relationship with parents, a realistic view of the teen's capacities, practical plans and goals for the future, and a firm sexual identity. At some point or other, it may also include an increasingly clear set of moral standards and spiritual life.

During this process of *identity consolidation*, teenagers actively experiment with a variety of identities and identifications. They try on miscellaneous styles, associate with and date different kinds of people, investigate various interests, and consider an array of goals and paths. Only after a period of exploration and experimentation can they evolve an enduring sense of self and a system of behavior, values, and goals to serve them in adulthood. They usually ape their parents in outward behavior after all.

During the course of identity exploration, the way a teenager thinks about the world, selects people to associate with, and chooses activities and occupations to engage in may undergo a series of noticeable changes. This is all in the service of learning and making internal adjustments.

Many of a youngster's beliefs and patterns have been adopted from his parents. These, too, now must be examined and reconsidered. Without such investigation, it is doubtful that a young person will find such adult roles as worker, adult, sibling, husband, or wife satisfying.

David B. Pruitt

No Longer a Teenager

my daughter, who turns twenty tomorrow,
has become truly independent.
she doesn't need her father to help her
deal with the bureaucracies of schools,
hmo's, insurance, the dmv.
she is quite capable of handling
landlords, bosses, and auto repair shops.
also boyfriends and roommates.
and her mother.

frankly it's been a big relief.
the teenage years were often stressful.
sometimes, though, i feel a little useless.

but when she drove down from northern California
to visit us for a couple of days,
she came through the door with the

biggest, warmest hug in the world for me.
and when we all went out for lunch,
she said, affecting a little girl's voice,
"i'm going to sit next to my daddy,"
and she did, and slid over close to me
so i could put my arm around her shoulder
until the food arrived.

i've been keeping busy since she's been gone,
mainly with my teaching and writing,
a little travel connected with both,
but i realized now how long it had been
since i had felt deep emotion.

when she left i said, simply,
"i love you,"
and she replied, quietly,
"i love you too."
you know it isn't always easy for
a twenty-year-old to say that;
it isn't always easy for a father.

literature and opera are full of
characters who die for love:
i stay alive for her.

GERALD I. LOCKLIN

That the world can be improved and yet must be celebrated as it is
are contradictions. The beginning of maturity may be the recognition
that both are true.

WILLIAM STOTT

When you were a child, you got report cards filled out by teachers to tell your parents how you were doing in school. It's difficult to make the transition from external judgment to internal acceptance, but it's a journey we all must make to reach our essential selves as adults.

Authentic success is internal. Often, other people aren't even aware at first that you've reached it. The moment of success is the awareness that "I can do it" or "I have done it." And it's comforting to know that this can't be taken away from you by an external event. Not by someone divorcing you, not by someone firing you.

When we achieve authentic success, we don't compare ourselves to others quite so often. That awful force, envy, seems to diminish. In fact, we want others to have the same chances we've had, to do what they would truly love to do. We become generous of spirit.

SARAH BAN BREATHNACH

Eventually, the mature person has come to the point where he is his own mother and his own father. He has, as it were, a motherly and a fatherly conscience. Motherly conscience says: "There is no misdeed, no crime which could deprive you of my love, of my wish for your life and happiness." Fatherly conscience says: "You did wrong, you cannot avoid accepting certain consequences of your wrongdoing, and most of all you must change your ways if I am to like you." The mature person has become free from the outside mother and father figures, and has built them up inside. In contrast to Freud's concept of the super-ego, however, he has built them inside not by *incorporating* mother and father, but by building a motherly conscience on his own capacity for love, and a fatherly conscience on his reason and judgment. Furthermore, the mature person loves with both the motherly and the fatherly conscience, in spite of the fact that they seem to contradict each other. If he would only retain his fatherly conscience, he would become harsh and inhuman. If he would only retain his motherly conscience, he would be apt to lose judgment and to hinder himself and others in their development.

In this development from mother-centered to father-centered attachment, and their eventual synthesis, lies the basis for mental health and the achievement of maturity.

ERICH FROMM

In this process of moving away, we negotiate our particular individual identities by bumping into different people or groups and by comparing ourselves with them. The conversation with our past continues, but we now add new conversational partners. Some of them affirm our childhood identity. Others contribute new ideas and roles.

ROBERT WUTHNOW

It is natural to think that moral maturity follows the same growth patterns as does physical or social/intellectual maturity. Many assume that, since a child tends to mature in each of these categories just before entrance to adulthood, personal morality follows suit. This is not so. Such thinking actually delays moral maturity by removing from parents a sense of urgency. Childhood is the period for imparting moral instruction and directing moral training, but please note that adolescence is when principles of right living, thinking, and acting should be realized.

In the Christian context, moral maturity (thinking and acting in harmony with God's moral law) should show itself between the ages of thirteen and fifteen. By the time children reach the teen years, they should have begun acquiring a moral code to which they adhere with increasing frequency. Adherence is dependent upon three things: moral knowledge (what does God's moral law say?), moral reason (what does the law mean?), and parental example (how valid is the law in the life of those insisting on it?). Moral maturity means your teen not only knows right from wrong, but he or she also knows why right is right and wrong is wrong.

GARY EZZO AND ANNE MARIE EZZO

The most important cognitive changes during early adolescence relate to the increasing ability of children to think abstractly, consider the hypothetical as well as the real, consider multiple dimensions of a problem at the same time, and reflect on themselves and on complicated problems. There is also a steady increase in the sophistication of children's information-processing and learning skills, their knowledge of different subjects, their ability to apply their knowledge to new learning situations, and their awareness of their own strengths and weaknesses as learners. These higher-order cognitive abilities help adolescents regulate their learning and behavior better to accomplish more complicated and elaborate tasks.

The same cognitive changes can also affect children's self-concepts, thoughts about their future, and understanding of others. During early adolescence, young people focus more on understanding the internal psychological characteristics of others, and they increasingly base their friendships on perceived compatibility in such personal characteristics. The middle-childhood and early-adolescent years are viewed by developmental psychologists as a time of change in the way children view themselves, as they consider what possibilities are available to them and try to come to a deeper understanding of themselves and others around them.

JACQUELYNNE S. ECCLES

In the United States, there is no consensus as to when an adolescent becomes an adult. The federal government determines the age at which one can vote and enter military service. Different religions select certain birthdays as the time to mark the passage from childhood to adult status. States have varying ages at which a teen can drive or drink. Our legal system can declare a teen an "emancipated minor" when it is clear that the teen wants to be financially and psychologically independent of family, thus making the teen—rather than the parents—responsible for his or her behavior. Some people think marriage confers adult status, others think that giving birth or fathering children makes them adults. Some think it happens when they move out of a parent's home, others think that teens become adults when they enter the job market and obtain part-time or full-time employment, making it possible for them to be financially independent of their families regardless of their actual ages.

However, external factors such as age, place of abode, or financial independence really offer little insight about when an adolescent becomes an adult because they don't tell us whether psychological independence has been achieved.

ROBERT C. KOLODNY ET AL.

Public, private, and secret levels of ritual often intertwine. Many of the moments of secret passage preview the private and public rites of passage.

In the spring of my twelfth year, my mother thought I was finally old enough to be trusted to go downtown and back on the bus alone. She didn't know I was already way beyond buses. I had been driving her car around the neighborhood when she was away from home.

The rite of passage was in that scary moment—the first time I started the car, shifted into gear, and rolled off down the street thinking: *I am going to die.* And: *She is going to kill me.* And: *Ohmygod I'm driving!*

I went around the block only once. But that was enough. When I had safely parked the car in the driveway, I sat very still in the driver's seat, holding on to the wheel for a long time. A scared kid got into the car when this adventure began. When the door opened next, a *driver* got out—one who was driven to go on to whatever came next in the passages of autonomy.

I had passed over from one stage of life to another.

From child in danger to dangerous child.

When my father finally got around to teaching me to drive, he was impressed at my "natural" talent for driving. When I took my test and got my license and my father gave me my own set of keys to the car one night at dinner, it was a major rite of passage for him and my mother. Their perception of me had changed and was formally acknowledged. For me the occasion meant a *private* sanction to do in *public* what I had already been doing in *secret*.

The private family passage into a public status had been presaged by that secret first drive of terror and joy. No parent can provide that moment, and no civil authority can license it; but nothing can match it in one's memory. The shift of self-perception is the most powerful ingredient in the chain reaction of becoming the person you are always becoming.

ROBERT FULGHUM

Adolescence is a time when we experience a spiritual hunger which is often misunderstood as restlessness, frustration, or anger. When we acknowledge this ripe sacred yearning, the teen years can be seen as a time of possibilities and expansion. Our sons and daughters are on the brink of discovering their vast potential and feel this calling, although it is often blurred and confused by the pull of the culture in which they live and the bodies that house their spirits.

Daily pressures can seem overwhelming: peer influences, the hazards of substance abuse and sexual activity, the risks and freedoms of driving and dating, the pressure to succeed in school and get into a good college. We want to help our teens meet these challenges and enter the world as successful, confident young adults. We advise, warn, help with algebra, turn over our car keys, wait up into the wee hours, and travel to college campuses. However, we may be missing the core component for helping our teens develop into healthy and competent adults—nurturing their spirituality.

Spirituality can be thought of as a positive sense of life purpose and a feeling of hope for one's future. Spirituality is a connection with a power greater than ourselves and with all creation. The process we follow as we quest for more knowledge of what is inside and outside of ourselves is our "spiritual journey." Jamie, a fifteen-year-old ripe with a soulful curiosity says it well: "What I'm figuring out is: How do I *do* my life?"

You are able to contribute to your teenage children's spirituality in ways more profound than you ever imagined. It's as simple as choosing to love them more deeply in the midst of the ordinary: replacing irritation with understanding, suggesting options rather than insisting upon specific solutions, and focusing on their beautiful inner light rather than on annoying behaviors. Nurturing a teenager's spirituality should become as integral a part of parenting as setting a curfew and requiring the use of seat belts.

Two questions consume teens: "Who am I?" and "Where do I fit in?" Although they may look for answers in decidedly nonspiritual places, their search for an identity and home in this world is a spiritual quest. Spirituality provides meaning to life. It fuels self-worth, a sense of purpose and guides us toward behaviors that honor the Divine spark in others and ourselves.

MIMI DOE

The Day Zimmer Lost Religion

The first Sunday I missed Mass on purpose
I waited all day for Christ to climb down
Like a wiry flyweight from the cross and
Club me on my irreverent teeth, to wade into
My blasphemous gut and drop me like a
Red hot thurible, the devil roaring in
Reserved seats until he got the hiccups.

It was a long cold way from the old days
When cassocked and surpliced I mumbled Latin
At the old priest and rang his obscure bell.
A long way from the dirty wind that blew
The soot like venial sins across the schoolyard
Where God reigned as a threatening,
One-eyed triangle high in the fleecy sky.

The first Sunday I missed Mass on purpose
I waited all day for Christ to climb down
Like the playground bully, the cuts and mice
Upon his face agleam, and pound me
Till my irreligious tongue hung out.
But of course He never came, knowing that
I was grown up and ready for Him now.

Paul Zimmer

August said, "Listen to me now, Lily. I'm going to tell you something I want you always to remember, all right?"

Her face had grown serious. Intent. Her eyes did not blink.

"All right," I said, and I felt something electric slide down my spine.

"Our Lady is not some magical being out there somewhere, like a fairy godmother. She's not the statue in the parlor. She's something inside of you. Do you understand what I'm telling you?"

"Our Lady is inside me," I repeated, not sure I did.

"You have to find a mother inside yourself. We all do. Even if we already have a mother, we still have to find this part of ourselves inside."

Sue Monk Kidd

Today you can look back and see the "child you" off in the distance— no longer your life, but a memory. Your parents can look ahead and imagine the crossroads you will soon stand at as you wave goodbye and go off to college or to travel overseas or to pursue your dreams.

One version of you flows into another. No traveling ghostlike figure follows and observes you, but every once in a while you can step back and look at your life as an outsider might. Right now you would see yourself moving off the path of childhood and onto the path leading to the "adult you."

Lynn M. Acquafondata

In fact, the search for individual identity is far more promising in concept than it is in actuality. Most answers in response to the question "Who am I?" load the coffers of our understanding with fool's gold. This is because "Who am I?" is an adolescent question.

Adolescence is not a bad thing, by the way. It consists in breaking free. Adolescents jump from goal to goal, responding to this stimulus or that, embracing one idea and then another. Adolescents are "indiscriminate evaluators." Over time, we winnow our experiments into more sustained endeavors—often from many sexual relationships to one dedicated relationship, from many vocational possibilities to a single job, from quicksilver intellectual passions to a more sustained set of values about the world and our place in it. At the end of this process, and for very good reason, ideally we will ask, "How am I doing?" and "How can I do it better?" rather than waste time pondering who we are.

FORREST CHURCH

Youth should be kept strangers to all that is bad, and especially to things which suggest vice or hate. When the five years have passed away, during the two following years they must look on at the pursuits which they are hereafter to learn. There are two periods of life with reference to which education has to be divided, from seven to the age of puberty, and onwards to the age of one and twenty.

ARISTOTLE

In the transition we call coming of age, we see the child trying to hold on to the true self and actively creating, at the same time, the self who will become the adult. Everything is in flux, and it will be for a while. But there is something that comes from taking all that energy, chaos, and flux and shaping it into a statement, a service, and a celebration that will go with them as they grow—something that says that being whole is a collaborative act, requiring us to hold on to our true selves and also to each other.

JUDITH E. MEYER

We become male automatically because of the Y chromosome and the little magic peanut, but if we are to become men we need the help of other men—we need our fathers to model for us and then to anoint us, we need our buddies to share the coming-of-age rituals with us and to let us join the team of men, and we need myths of heroes to inspire us and to show us the way.

FRANK PITTMAN

It is a matter of transitions, you see; the changing, the becoming must be cared for closely.

LESLIE MARMON SILKO

Passage

Young woman,
Young man,
Life turns for you.

This is a magic time,
    a mythic passage,
In your becoming.

We who welcome you,
None of us is too old
So as to have forgotten
        —the mystery of not
        knowing,
        —the delight of first
        discovery,
        —the impatience to hurry
        what will come next,
        —the terrible wonderfulness
        of the changes.

Don't forget.
We remember.
And with memory and hope
We welcome you,
Knowing what you may become

Is a bud
Bursting into a flower
Just now.

To you,
    young man,
To you,
    young woman.
We wish
    all the mystery,
    all the discovery,
    all the moments,
    all the changes
That are yours.
We can't give them;
For they are yours
To take!

EDWARD SEARL

Do you remember that moment in your early teens when the adults whom you grew up around really saw that glimmer in you of what was to come? Or when you first did something that impressed the adults, and it gave you the first taste of what it feels like to be acknowledged as a person, regardless of your age? This is a moment of coming of age, when you become aware of the extent of your own worth and dignity as a human being by way of the world simply noticing you.

Coming of age. It's part of coming to our full humanity, of claiming our promise.

HANNAH WELLS

The fundamental fact about our experience is that it is a process of change.

WILLIAM JAMES

You

Out of nothing there comes a time called childhood, which is simply a path leading through an archway called adolescence. A small town there, past the arch called youth.

Soon, down the road, where one almost misses the life lived beyond the flower, is a small shack labeled, you.

And it is here the future lives in the several postures of arm on windowsill, cheek on this; elbows on knees, face in the hands; sometimes the head thrown back, eyes staring into the ceiling . . . . This into nothing down the long day's arc . . . .

RUSSELL EDSON

That Crazy Cliff

Anyway, I keep picturing all these little kids playing some game in this big field of rye and all. Thousands of little kids, and nobody's around—nobody big, I mean—except me. And I'm standing on the edge of some crazy cliff. What I have to do, I have to catch everybody if they start to go over the cliff—I mean if they're running and they don't look where they're going I have to come out from somewhere and catch them. That's all I do all day. I'd just be the catcher in the rye and all. I know it's crazy, but that's the only thing I'd really like to be.

J. D. Salinger

Coming of age never really ends. It is a regenerative and cyclic process, moving a bit forward, a bit back, seeming more an adult one minute, less so another.

We are children forever, but as adults of whatever faith suits us, we accept the joys and responsibilities of adulthood. We come to terms with the potential for sorrow and loss, for love and continuity, for solitude and community, for vulnerability and strength. And most important, we promise to take care of those coming of age after us—not necessarily catching them, perhaps, but cushioning them a bit as they fall off that crazy cliff to adulthood.

Susan Morrison Hebble

Pushing 7 ½, Falling into 8

Tonight, we lie on his bed
and he cries, "I'm ugly."
And I try to hold him,
try to rock him, but he's all new,
with his long arms and hairy legs.
And I find that at seven-and-a-half
there is nothing small left
for me to comfort.
He turns away from me and cries
from a place so deep inside
that there is no sound,
until the pain reaches his throat,
and he says, "Mama, I don't want to be me,
I want to be a baby again."
Does it matter that he doesn't listen
to me anymore?
Before bed he looked into the mirror
at the two teeth pushing from
his lower gum, crowding the wobbly
baby teeth that refuse to leave.
I told him, "You're so handsome."
"No, I'm not." he said and stared
at the rows of tiny teeth.
"But you are." I said.
"Mama," he replied, "I can see."

Tonight, I try to hold on to him
and a tear drops into his ear.
"What was that?" he asks.
His dog at the foot of the bed lifts its head,
our cat stands up and stretches her long body.
All three unaware that I am falling
off the edge of this bed.
That there is no room for me anymore.
And that this is new to me—
this falling.

VICKI WHICKER

My Middle Daughter, on the Edge of Adolescence, Learns to Play the Saxophone

for Rebecca

Her hair, that halo of red gold curls,
has thickened, coarsened,
lost its baby fineness,
and the sweet smell of childhood
that clung to her clothes
has just about vanished.
Now she's getting moody,
moaning about her hair,

clothes that aren't the right brands,
boys that tease.
She clicks over the saxophone keys
with gritty fingernails polished in pink pearl,
grass stains on the knees
of her sister's old designer jeans.
She's gone from sounding like the smoke detector
through Old MacDonald and Jingle Bells.
Soon she'll master these keys,
turn notes into liquid gold,
wail that reedy brass.
Soon, she'll be a woman.
She's gonna learn to play the blues.

BARBARA CROOKER

Adolescence is a tough time for parent and child alike. It is a time between: between childhood and maturity, between parental protection and personal responsibility, between life stage-managed by grown-ups and life privately held.

ANNA QUINDLEN

Starting in 1991, Dr. Jay Giedd, chief of brain imaging at the Child Psychiatry Branch of the National Institute of Mental Health (NIMH), started taking pictures of kids' brains over a nine-year span. He was curious to know to what extent children's crazy behavior is willful, and to what extent it is beyond their control. He and his colleagues at UCLA and McGill University in Canada used magnetic resonance imaging (MRI) to study exactly how a child's brain grows from ages 3 to 18. They studied almost 1,000 "normal" kids (including two of Dr. Giedd's children) at intervals ranging from two weeks to four years. What they found was nothing short of astonishing, and it completely rewrote our understanding of the adolescent brain.

First, contrary to previous thinking that the brain is completely developed by age five, they saw that throughout the teen years and into the twenties, substantial growth occurs in a brain structure called the corpus callosum. The corpus callosum is a set of nerves that connects all the parts of the brain that must work together to function efficiently, as in making good decisions. This set of "wires" is critical to things like intelligence, consciousness, and self-awareness. This initial finding was revolutionary enough, but these researchers weren't finished.

With amazement, they also found that the prefrontal cortex of the brain goes through a wild growth spurt that coincides with the onset of adolescence. In fact, they found that this part of the brain does the bulk of its maturation between the ages of 12 and 20. The prefrontal cortex is where the most sophisticated of our abilities reside. Emotional control, impulse restraint, and rational decision-making are all gifts to us from our prefrontal cortex, gifts your kid hasn't yet received. Perhaps Dr. Karl Pribram, director of the Center for Brain Research and Informational Sciences at Radford University in Virginia, described it best when he said, "The prefrontal cortex is the seat of civilization."

MICHAEL J. BRADLEY

As a teenager relinquishes the emotional investment in the roles of childhood, there may be an accompanying sense of acute discomfort, confusion, and loss. The teen is no longer a child. The old manner of relating to parents, siblings, friends, and mentors no longer works. Old interests, activities, and involvements may seem immature and irrelevant. The teen will likely experience considerable anxiety until a comfortable new sense of self evolves.

DAVID B. PRUITT

The executive brain doesn't hit adult levels until the age of 25. At puberty, you have adult passions, sex drive, energy, and emotion, but the reining in doesn't happen until much later. We can vote at 18 and drive a car. But you can't rent a car until you're 25. In terms of brain anatomy, the only ones who have it right are the car-rental people.

JAY GIEDD

Adolescence is society's permission slip for combining physical maturity with psychological irresponsibility.

TERRI APTER

When a boy reaches adolescence, he discovers a new world, charged with power he hadn't been aware of before. He is drawn to it as though it were part of who he must become, and in a way it is. But he's far too young to handle it, and the experience of this new super-charged world makes an impression and issues a call that may be part of the rest of his life. The question of what must be done with that power will be with him until he resolves it.

DAVIDSON LOEHR

Are you there God? It's me, Margaret. I just told my mother I want a bra. Please help me grow God. You know where. I want to be like everyone else.

JUDY BLUME

Adolescence II

Although it is night, I sit in the bathroom, waiting.
Sweat prickles behind my knees, the baby-breasts are alert.
Venetian blinds slice up the moon; the tiles quiver in pale strips.

Then they come, the three seal men with eyes as round
As dinner plates and eyelashes like sharpened tines.
They bring the scent of licorice. One sits in the washbowl,

One on the bathtub edge; one leans against the door.
"Can you feel it yet?" they whisper.
I don't know what to say, again. They chuckle,

Patting their sleek bodies with their hands.
"Well, maybe next time." And they rise,
Glittering like pools of ink under moonlight,

And vanish. I clutch at the ragged holes
They leave behind, here at the edge of darkness.
Night rests like a ball of fur on my tongue.

RITA DOVE

Puppy Called Puberty

It was like keeping a puppy in your underpants
A secret puppy you weren't allowed to show to anyone
Not even your best friend or your worst enemy

You wanted to pat him stroke him cuddle him
All the time but you weren't supposed to touch him

He only slept for five minutes at a time
Then he'd suddenly perk up his head
In the middle of school medical inspection
And always on bus rides

So you had to climb down from the upper deck
All bent double to smuggle the puppy off the bus
Without the buxom conductress spotting
Your wicked and ticketless stowaway.

Jumping up, wet-nosed, eagerly wagging—
He only stopped being a nuisance
When you were alone together
Pretending to be doing your homework
But really gazing at each other
Through hot and hazy daydreams

Of those beautiful schoolgirls on the bus
With kittens bouncing in their sweaters.

ADRIAN MITCHELL

So what would happen if suddenly, magically, men could menstruate and women could not?

Clearly, menstruation would become an enviable, boast-worthy, masculine event:

Men would brag about how long and how much.

Young boys would talk about it as the envied beginning of manhood. Gifts, religious ceremonies, family dinners, and stag parties would mark the day.

GLORIA STEINEM

Snow White's Acne

At first she was sure it was just a bit of dried strawberry juice, or a fleck of her mother's red nail polish that had flaked off when she'd patted her daughter to sleep the night before. But as she scrubbed, Snow felt a bump, something festering under the surface, like a tapeworm curled up and living in her left cheek.

Doc the Dwarf was no dermatologist and besides Snow doesn't get to meet him in this version because the mint leaves the tall doctor puts over her face only make matters worse. Snow and the Queen hope against hope for chicken pox, measles, something that would be gone quickly and not plague Snow's whole adolescence.

If only freckles were red, she cried, if only concealer really worked. Soon came the pus, the yellow dots, multiplying like pins in a pin cushion. Soon came the greasy hair. The Queen gave her daughter a razor for her legs and a stick of underarm deodorant.

Snow doodled through her teenage years—"Snow + ?" in Magic Markered hearts all over her notebooks. She was an average student, a daydreamer who might have been a scholar if she'd only applied herself. She liked sappy music and romance novels. She liked pies and cake instead of fruit.

The Queen remained the fairest in the land. It was hard on Snow, having such a glamorous mom. She rebelled by wearing torn shawls and baggy gowns. Her mother would sometimes say, "Snow darling, why don't you pull back your hair? Show those pretty eyes?" or "Come on, I'll take you shopping."

Snow preferred staying in her safe room, looking out of her window at the deer leaping across the lawn. Or she'd practice her dance moves with invisible princes. And the Queen, busy being Queen, didn't like to push it.

DENISE DUHAMEL

43

Virgin Youth

Now and again
All my body springs alive,
And the life that is polarised in my eyes,
That quivers between my eyes and mouth,
Flies like a wild thing across my body,
Leaving my eyes half-empty, and clamorous,
Filling my still breasts with a flush and a flame,
Gathering the soft ripples below my breasts
Into urgent, passionate waves,
And my soft, slumbering belly
Quivering awake with one impulse of desire,
Gathers itself fiercely together;
And my docile, fluent arms
Knotting themselves with wild strength
To clasp—what they have never clasped.
Then I tremble, and go trembling
Under the wild, strange tyranny of my body,
Till it has spent itself,
And the relentless nodality of my eyes reasserts itself,
Till the bursten flood of life ebbs back to my eyes,
Back from my beautiful, lonely body
Tired and unsatisfied.

D. H. Lawrence

I walked home and threw my backpack on the floor of my room next to a pile of dirty clothes. To the untrained eye, my room was a mess. I, however, knew where everything was. There was a pile of recycled materials for collages. Next to that were my sketches and notes. After peeling off my school clothes and throwing them in the dirty clothes pile, I noticed a bright red spot on my underpants.

What a shock. It had happened. Ahead of schedule like my precocious breasts.

Thinking my mother would never believe me without physical evidence, I rushed up to the kitchen.

"Look, Mom," I announced, presenting her with the underpants.

"Well, what a surprise. Your sister hasn't even gotten her period yet."

Boy, will she be mad, I fretted, genuinely worried. Joe is two and a half years older than me and this was the first time I had ever accomplished something before she had; at least getting my period felt like an accomplishment.

My mother took me to her bathroom, closed the door, and began going through the mechanics of how to attach a sanitary napkin to its support belt. These were back in the days before maxi pads.

"I was going to get you girls your own supply of sanitary napkins so you'd have them when the time came, but you beat me to it."

What? So we'd just get our periods and use this stuff without telling you? Wouldn't you want to know the moment we became women?

And that's how it was at my house: no fanfare. In fact, after that brief discussion, it was rarely mentioned unless I needed some more supplies from the grocery store. My sister was not storming around the house slamming doors, so apparently my mom didn't give her the news. My father must have known, but you never would have guessed it by looking at his face at dinner. It was just a secret between my mother and me, an embarrassing secret.

My mother confessed that I was entering a "difficult age." The carefree days of childhood were over. My parents were to become more and more uncomfortable with me as I awakened to my own sexuality.

KAREN MURPHY

The first time he had an orgasm the boy very nearly tumbled off the top plank of the barnyard fence. He was through with his Saturday chores, it was too early to milk, and he had just finished reading, with virtue and relief, the last chapter of the Book of Ezekiel. It was late March and the sun was shining, but such a wild wind was scouring across the farm that he was obliged to wear his mackinaw and his leather aviation helmet.

When he climbed the fence to check on the baby pigs, he discovered a secluded spot next to the barn wall that was out of the wind and deliciously warmed by the reflected sun. He rested snugly there, content in the idle joy of an undemanding moment. Perched eight feet above the ground, he listened to the rich soughing of the wind roaring over the barn, watched a sun-glinted buzzard scud in lean and stiffened control across the rapid sky, breathed the vaguely spicy, musty smell of dried horse manure, and became aware of an impelling erection.

Idly he unbuttoned his overalls and slowly began the puerile manipulation. He concentrated on interpreting his afternoon reading, assuming that the Lord would be so interested in his thoughts that He would ignore his hand. For long moments he pondered and played. He noted that the buzzard had wheeled in the opposite direction and now hung, much higher and almost stationary, facing the wind. The boy envied the bird. Of a sudden he became absolutely inundated with sensation. His toes curled upward against his shoes, his elbows and upper stomach tingled, and then irresistible force came tearing and shocking in overwhelming pulsations through his loins. His mind was already on Ezekiel, and he saw myriad golden wheels spinning within wheels, covered with eyes and surrounded by coals of fire. He thought he must have a lightning rod in his lap, but the lightning was coming from within him. His hat fell into the barn lot, and he clung dizzily to the plank with both hands until his body shuddered into immobility and relaxed.

"Good Lord! What in the world was that?" he cried aloud. He suddenly realized that he was out in the open, full under the gaze of Jehovah Himself and indeed in direct communication with Him. There was no way to hide this from the Lord. He was no smarter than Adam after all. His fig leaf had even slipped. He glanced around to be sure there had been no human witness to this sensual cataclysm. Only the buzzard was watching, and it appeared unbelievably disinterested, still intent on balance and glide. He was not surprised to note that the wind had stilled. That seemed fitting.

As he climbed down the fence and retrieved his cap from the attention of a curious pig, he identified again with Adam and his humiliating expulsion from the Garden.

FERROL SAMS

Adolescence

There was a time when in late afternoon
The four-o'clocks would fold up at day's close,
Pink-white in prayer. Under the floating moon
I lay with them in calm and sweet repose.

And in the open spaces I could sleep,
Half-naked to the shining worlds above;
Peace came with sleep and sleep was long and deep,
Gained without effort, sweet like early love.

But now no balm—nor drug nor weed nor wine—
Can bring true rest to cool my body's fever,
Nor sweeten in my mouth the acid brine,
That salts my choicest drink and will forever.

CLAUDE MCKAY

I would there were no age between sixteen and three-and-twenty, or that youth would sleep out the rest; for there is nothing in the between but getting wenches with child, wronging the ancientry, stealing, fighting.

WILLIAM SHAKESPEARE

Our beliefs about teenagers are deeply contradictory: They should be free to become themselves. They need many years of training and study. They know more about the future than adults do. They know hardly anything at all. They ought to know the value of a dollar. They should be protected from the world of work. They are frail, vulnerable creatures. They are children. They are sex fiends. They are the death of culture. They are the hope of us all.

We love the idea of youth, but are prone to panic about the young. The very qualities that adults find exciting and attractive about teenagers are entangled with those we find terrifying. Their energy threatens anarchy. Their physical beauty and budding sexuality menaces moral standards. Their assertion of physical and intellectual power makes their parents at once proud and painfully aware of their own mortality.

These qualities—the things we love, fear, and think we know about the basic nature of young people—constitute a teenage mystique: a seductive but damaging way of understanding young people. This mystique encourages adults to see teenagers (and young people to see themselves) not as individuals but as potential problems. Such a pessimistic view of the young can easily lead adults to feel that they are powerless to help young people make better lives for themselves. Thus, the teenage mystique can serve as an excuse for elders to neglect the coming generation and, ultimately, to see their worst fears realized.

THOMAS HINE

All over Harlem, Negro boys and girls are growing into stunted maturity, trying desperately to find a place to stand; and the wonder is not that so many are ruined but that so many survive.

JAMES BALDWIN

You just can't predict the course of friendship among girls at this age. There's a need—varying in intensity according to the individual— for Gibraltar-like attachments in this betwixt-and-between period. Impressive sophistication and maturity exist side by side with fear-some anxiety about the changing body, the person-to-be. The "best friends" are anchors against these tides of confusion.

STELLA CHESS AND JANE WHITBREAD

My son, 17, turns 18 this Sunday. He skipped school today. I found him swinging in the hammock, his face as gray as the June Gloom filling our sky.

"Mom, I haven't done anything with my life."

He didn't look at me, spoke to the backyard, and I remembered being young and serious and dramatic. I started reciting a list of all the ways he makes my life better, but I caught myself, stopped. Almost 18-year-olds don't need a litany of a mom's memories. I rubbed his hair and stepped back into the house.

It's tough being 17. It's tough being 18. I didn't want to tell my boy that it's tough being 39, too, tough in well-worn ways. I poured a tall glass of water and sat at the kitchen table to flip through today's newspaper. Mudslide. Spelling Bee champion. Deep Throat. What a world, I thought. I took a sip of water. I turned the page. An article caught my eye. Rock and Roll Marathon this Sunday. Hmmmmmm. A half hour later my son and I hugged. We will run and walk 26.2 miles through San Diego together this Sunday morning to celebrate his rite of passage. He will start as my young boy and cross the finish line a grown man, and along the way, at every mile, a rock and roll band will serenade us. I'm not hawking Avon this race. I'm not going to wear my crazy kilt or convince fellow runners to try some Skin So Soft. I'm just going to run with my boy. Maybe we'll talk about life.

BIRDIE JAWORSKI

Prepping the Children

don't give your brood
too much information
let them find out for themselves
no matter how rude and disturbing
let the story unwind naturally
though, as a caring parent,
the inclination is to try and prepare them
for the traumas that lie ahead

this was quite apparent
when our local cinema
double featured Bambi and Snow White
almost from the first frame
there was a constant undercurrent
of anxious little voices asking
"Is this where Bambi's mother is shot?"
"Is this where the wicked witch appears?"

if you overly prepare your children
for the tragedies up ahead
they might not be able
to enjoy the show
wouldn't it be unsettling if
in the theater of real life
your offspring were constantly

tugging on your sleeve asking
"Is this where daddy cheats on mommy?"
"Is this where the accident happens?"
"Is this where grandpa dies?"

let a story unfold naturally
before their innocent eyes
let the dwarfs whistle while they work
let Thumper and Bambi play
let the twists and turns
just around the corner
come as a surprise

Ric Masten

If youth is the season of hope, it is often so only in the sense that our elders are hopeful about us; for no age is so apt as youth to think its emotions, partings, and resolves are the last of their kind. Each crisis seems final, simply because it is new.

George Eliot

It's also a particularly cruel irony of nature, I think, that right at this time when the brain is most vulnerable is also the time when teens are most likely to experiment with drugs or alcohol. Sometimes when I'm working with teens, I actually show them these brain development curves, how they peak at puberty and then prune down and try to reason with them that if they're doing drugs or alcohol that evening, it may not just be affecting their brains for that night or even for that weekend, but for the next 80 years of their life.

JAY GIEDD

It might sound a paradoxical thing to say—for surely never has a generation of children occupied more sheer hours of parental time—but the truth is that we neglected you. We allowed you a charade of trivial freedoms in order to avoid making those impositions on you that are in the end both the training ground and proving ground for true independence. We pronounced you strong when you were still weak in order to avoid the struggles with you that would have fed your true strength. We proclaimed you sound when you were foolish in order to avoid taking part in the long, slow, slogging effort that is the only route to genuine maturity of mind and feeling. Thus, it was no small anomaly of your growing up that while you were the most indulged generation, you were also in many ways the most abandoned to your own meager devices by those into whose safe-keeping you had been given.

MIDGE DECTER

Adolescents need to be reassured that nothing—neither their growing maturity, their moods, their misbehavior, nor your anger at something they have done—can shake your basic commitment to them.

LAURENCE STEINBERG AND ANN LEVINE

The age of puberty is a crisis in the life of the man worth studying. It is the passage from the Unconscious to the Conscious; from the sleep of the Passions to their rage; from careless receiving to cunning providing; from beauty to use; from omnivorous curiosity to anxious stewardship; from faith to doubt; from maternal Reason to hard short-sighted Understanding; from Unity to disunion; the progressive influences of poetry, eloquence, love, regeneration, character, truth, sorrow, and of search for an Aim, & the contest for Property.

RALPH WALDO EMERSON

And when will you exist?—Oh, it is I,
Incredibly skinny, stooped, and neat as pie,
Ignorant as dirt, erotic as an ape,
Dreamy as puberty—with dirty hair!

KARL SHAPIRO

Ground Swell

Is nothing real but when I was fifteen,
Going on sixteen, like a corny song?
I see myself so clearly then, and painfully—
Knees bleeding through my usher's uniform
Behind the candy counter in the theater
After a morning's surfing; paddling frantically
To top the brisk outsiders coming to wreck me,
Trundle me clumsily along the beach floor's
Gravel and sand; my knees aching with salt.
Is that all I have to write about?
You write about the life that's vividest.
And if that is your own, that is your subject.
And if the years before and after sixteen
Are colorless as salt and taste like sand—
Return to those remembered chilly mornings,
The light spreading like a great skin on the water,
And the blue water scalloped with wind-ridges,
And—what was it exactly?—that slow waiting
When, to invigorate yourself, you peed
Inside your bathing suit and felt the warmth
Crawl all around your hips and thighs,
And the first set rolled in and the water level
Rose in expectancy, and the sun struck
The water surface like a brassy palm,
Flat and gonglike, and the wave face formed.

Yes. But that was a summer so removed
In time, so specially peculiar to my life,
Why would I want to write about it again?
There was a day or two when, paddling out,
An older boy who had just graduated
And grown a great blonde moustache, like a walrus,
Skimmed past me like a smooth machine on the water,
And said my name. I was so much younger,
To be identified by one like him—
The easy deference of a kind of god
Who also went to church where I did—made me
Reconsider my worth. I had been noticed.
He soon was a small figure crossing waves,
The shawling crest surrounding him with spray,
Whiter than gull feathers. He had said my name
Without scorn, just with a bit of surprise
To notice me among those trying the big waves
Of the morning break. His name is carved now
On the black wall in Washington, the frozen wave
That grievers cross to find a name or names.
I knew him as I say I knew him, then,
Which wasn't very well. My father preached
His funeral. He came home in a bag
That may have mixed in pieces of his squad.
Yes, I can write about a lot of things
Besides the summer that I turned sixteen.

But that's my ground swell. I must start
Where things began to happen and I knew it.

MARK JARMAN

Hanging Fire
I am fourteen
and my skin has betrayed me
the boy I cannot live without
still sucks his thumb
in secret
how come my knees are
always so ashy
what if I die
before morning
and momma's in the bedroom
with the door closed.

I have to learn how to dance
in time for the next party
my room is too small for me
suppose I die before graduation
they will sing sad melodies
but finally
tell the truth about me

There is nothing I want to do
and too much
that has to be done
and momma's in the bedroom
with the door closed.

Nobody even stops to think
about my side of it
I should have been on Math Team
my marks were better than his
why do I have to be
the one
wearing braces
I have nothing to wear tomorrow
will I live long enough
to grow up
and momma's in the bedroom
with the door closed.

AUDRE LORDE

An adolescent is both an impulsive child and a self-starting adult.

MASON COOLEY

Boyish Dreams of Manhood

Joey nearly topples under the weight of his aluminum bat
   as he swings

his office door closed with a sigh and, tossing cold takeout
   on his desk, he

Gallops across the dusty backyard, plastic silver gun gleaming
   in its holster, pulling

the knot of his tie straight before he enters the conference room,
   shaky about his

First sixth-grade dance, the one where he plans to ask Marjorie
   Coleman to

hold his calls—boss wants to see him—God, how he needs
   some antacid to settle

The score with Eddie, who pushes his glasses up on his nose
   while he talks, saying

it's the worst report he's ever seen come across his desk and
   maybe he ought to

Go outside and watch fire trucks roar past, waving at the men
   in hats who grin and

apologize, promising to do better next time, feeling his shirt collar
   grow warm
In the sunshine, sherbet dripping between his fingers, a Daddy
   Longlegs lazily dragging

his briefcase past the shiny black sports car to his own dusty
   wagon and opens

His sleeping bag with a whoosh! Lighting the coal oil lantern
   he giggles and munches on

the end of a cigarette, tapping his thumbs on the steering wheel
   in time to

The hush of ghost stories told on blankets of marshmallows,
   staying up all night to

rock the crying baby and send wide-eyed worries to the ceiling
   before

Morning comes and Mom brings hot cocoa and the boys hurry
   to get to practice and

briskly kisses his wife goodbye to start it all again. So much to do.
So much to do.

So much to do, but still Joey pauses a moment to imagine himself
as a grown man, he

pauses to remember himself as a little boy. He can almost feel the
holster warm on his hip.

JENNIFER BROWN

The Boy Was Young

The boy was young (your son, my son)
He held life,
gentle and fragile as a wren's spotted egg,
in play-black-lined hands.

He brought it to me.
His eyebrows asked: What?
How should this find,
this all-that-he-had
glistening in its bed of dark sweat
be used?
What does it mean
to hold your life with your fingers?

How should I tell him how to live?
How do you tell someone you love
    humanity is frail
    (as he is frail, as you are frail)
    and mistakes will be made
    and life is fitting parts that don't belong?

RUDOLPH NEMSER

So Full of Distance

Little Girl, My String Bean, My Lovely Woman

My daughter, at eleven
(almost twelve), is like a garden.

Oh, darling! Born in that sweet birthday suit
and having owned it and known it for so long,
now you must watch high noon enter—
noon, that ghost hour.
Oh, funny little girl—this one under a blueberry sky,
this one! How can I say that I've known
just what you know and just where you are?

It's not a strange place, this odd home
where your face sits in my hand
so full of distance,
so full of its immediate fever.
The summer has seized you,
as when, last month in Amalfi, I saw
lemons as large as your desk-side globe—
that miniature map of the world—
and I could mention, too,
the market stalls of mushrooms
and garlic buds all engorged.
Or I think even of the orchard next door,
where the berries are done
and the apples are beginning to swell.

And once, with our first backyard,
I remember I planted an acre of yellow beans
we couldn't eat.

Oh, little girl,
my stringbean,
how do you grow?
You grow this way.
You are too many to eat.

I hear
as in a dream
the conversation of the old wives
speaking of womanhood.
I remember that I heard nothing myself.
I was alone.
I waited like a target.

Let high noon enter—
the hour of the ghosts.
Once the Romans believed
that noon was the ghost hour,
and I can believe it, too,
under that startling sun,
and someday they will come to you,
someday, men bare to the waist, young Romans

at noon where they belong,
with ladders and hammers
while no one sleeps.

But before they enter
I will have said,
Your bones are lovely,
and before their strange hands
there was always this hand that formed.

Oh, darling, let your body in,
let it tie you in,
in comfort.
What I want to say, Linda,
is that women are born twice.

If I could have watched you grow
as a magical mother might,
if I could have seen through my magical transparent belly,
there would have been such a ripening within:
your embryo,
the seed taking on its own,
life clapping the bedpost,
bones from the pond,
thumbs and two mysterious eyes,
the awfully human head,

the heart jumping like a puppy,
the important lungs,
the becoming—
while it becomes!
as it does now,
a world of its own,
a delicate place.

I say hello
to such shakes and knockings and high jinks,
such music, such sprouts,
such dancing-mad-bears of music,
such necessary sugar,
such goings-on!

Oh, little girl,
my stringbean,
how do you grow?
You grow this way.
You are too many to eat.

What I want to say, Linda,
is that there is nothing in your body that lies.
All that is new is telling the truth.
I'm here, that somebody else,
an old tree in the background.

Darling,
stand still at your door,
sure of yourself, a white stone, a good stone—
as exceptional as laughter
you will strike fire,
that new thing!

ANNE SEXTON

For Stephen

Seventeen, no great event
He says. He glides past us
With undisturbed intent.

He would photograph well
Easing into the jeep
Whose military shell

He painted red to cover
The old green wounds,
That war long over.

This boy, this innocence,
Brown, summer muscle
Flexed without pretense.

There are no mysteries
For him. The winter branch
Always leafs into light.
Supreme biology.
His days shine with chance.

I follow his car in mine.
Dust rises from our road.
Three months without rain,
Already some of the pines

I planted a year ago
Are dead. When we reach
The highway, we go
Apart. Always the wrong time

To tell my son what I mean.
He doesn't see my wave.
When I was seventeen
I didn't look back either.

CHRISTOPHER BROOKHOUSE

Her Door

for my daughter Sara Marie

There was a time her door was never closed.
Her music box played "Für Elise" in plinks.
Her crib new-bought—I drew her sleeping there.

The little drawing sits beside my chair.
These days, she ornaments her hands with rings.
She's seventeen. Her door is one I knock.

There was a time I daily brushed her hair
By window light—I bathed her, in the sink
In sunny water, in the kitchen, there.

I've bought her several thousand things to wear,
And now this boy buys her silver rings.
He goes inside her room and shuts the door.

Those days, to rock her was a form of prayer.
She'd gaze at me, and blink, and I would sing
Of bees and horses, in the pasture, there.

The drawing sits as still as nap-time air—
Her curled-up hand—that precious line, her cheek . . .

Next year her door will stand, again, ajar
But she herself will not be living there.

MARY LEADER

Adolescence literally means "growing into maturity." An adolescent
is neither child nor adult and therein lies much of the difficulty, the
turbulence, the confusion and the challenge. They need us, yet need
to not need us. We are their best bet, yet their instincts are to resist
us. Unlike primitive cultures, our highly complex society requires a
lengthy adolescence with very few rites of passage. The task of turning
children into adults has never been more daunting!

GORDON NEUFELD

First Menstruation

I had been waiting
waiting for what felt like lifetimes.
When the first girls stayed out of the ocean
a few days a month, wore shorts instead of a swimsuit
I watched them enviously.
I even stayed out once in a while, pretending.

At last, finding blood on my panties
I carried them to my mother, hoping
unsure, afraid—Mom, is this it?

She gave me Kotex and belt
showed me how to wear it.
Dot Lutz was there, smiling, saying when her Bonnie
got her period, she told her
when you have questions, come to me, ask me.
You can ask a mother anything.

I felt so strange when she said that.
Mom didn't say anything.

The three of us
standing in the bedroom
me, the woman-child, standing with the older women
and the feeling
there once was a feeling
that should be here,
there once was a rite, a communion.

I said, yes, I'll ask my mother
but we all, except maybe Dot,
knew it wasn't true.

ELLEN BASS

Children, as they grow into adolescents, metamorphose from dogs into cats. Whereas children love to be companioned, play, get in your face, run around, and generally have a fun time, somehow they gradually become less interested in all those things. They shed their inveterately happy, energetic selves. It's as if in the first decade of parenting you have a puppy to take care of, a puppy who constantly expresses love for you and takes all the attention you can humanly muster. And then, somewhere in the second decade of parenting, the darling little creature becomes emotionally aloof, regularly retreats to his or her bedroom or friends, no longer likes being hugged or kissed goodnight, and wants full control over when and how to be interacted with by the parents.

If you've been the owner of a cat, as I have, you know that cats refuse to be told what to do. They strut away, sometimes contemptuously, when someone tries to give them attention. Cats often are very particular about for whom they'll show affection. I imagine many of you parents know this canine to feline shift.

ALAN TAYLOR

Moods (14 years old)
They say I have moods,
that I am moody.
Well, actually, I have only three moods—
neutral,

upset,
and very upset.

It's they that have the moods,
if that's what you call them—
Changing unpredictably;
one minute cheerful
the next irate,
then so sorry,
so forgiving,
impatient,
forgetful,
ignorant,
ignoring,
uninterested,
busy cooking,
loud,
laughing,
tired,
tapping,
singing,
driving me crazy.

SARA EPSTEIN

Edge of the Nest

Forty-five
I watch
My teenaged daughter
Run breathless
Into our house.
Refrigerator open,
She stops.
Turns to me
Eyes wide,
It's true, she says
My friends joke
I look just like you.
Could you get a different haircut?

Twenty-nine
I fold
Tiny white undershirts
In the second floor walkup
We rent in Belleville.
I pair
Tiny yellow booties
So everything will be ready
For this baby

For whom I will never
Be ready.
If time permits
I will get my hair cut.

JESSICA DE KONINCK

Alterations

For years the dress I sewed
fit flawlessly, wrapped her
in plush protection and comfortable
cascades of satin.

How it ballooned and billowed
whenever she twirled
like a sparkler lit
in white-laced laughter.

I thought I saw
it tuck a bit tighter to her teenage curves.
But I had left
a healthy seam allowance,

room to grow. And yet
these days, I can't pretend.
The fabric is faded. It binds in spots
whenever she makes a bold gesture.

She says it chafes her skin.
I try to smooth the wrinkles
under mothering hands,
but it just puckers more.

Some threads have pulled
under the strain.
Not ripped but frayed
in a way I can't mend

without the world noticing
my mistake. I stand by as she
seizes pins and needles
and cotton thread.

Without a pattern
she is suddenly her own
seamstress. I gather the
outgrown garment

to my face, breathe in
silky scents of
talcum, sky and puberty
and fold those years

into a tissue-lined box.
There is nothing left
to do but take up measuring
tape and scissors

and silently snip and stitch and hem
until in season
I fashion a brand new dress,
this time for me to wear.

WENDY H. GILL

This book was written for my sons, but also for parents whose own children, like mine, after a certain age do not welcome parental advice. Occasionally they may listen to another adult, which is why perhaps people should switch children with their neighbors and friends for a while in the teen years!

MARIAN WRIGHT EDELMAN

As My Daughter Bleeds, So Do I

As my daughter bleeds, so do I.
Arhythmically, through an elliptical lunar phase.
Her womb is learning its beat, while mine is
missing measures or coming in on the
wrong count.

With Ariel's first bicycle, I held the seat
until she learned to ride.
How quickly her body found its own balance
and moved away from me, independently.
I stood in the street holding onto her return.

On her first period, I held her close
and drew her a hot bath, suspending time.
Her womb was on its own now, in free flowing richness.
This was not a privilege I could take away from her.
I gave her pads for her bleeding seat.

Lately, I ride behind my daughter, pulled
by the secret song of her steady cycle, up
hills, past swings, past babies, past youth.
Our rhythm eases my unshed longings.
I pass the water bottle over to her, like a baton.

One day, anticipating red, only my daughter will bleed instead.
My womb will rest in full stop. Hers will accelerate on, and
perhaps she, too, will sleep with babies in her bed.
And then, only my heart will move blood
in syncopated red rushes of love.

VALERIE ROOT WOLPE

Happy is that mother whose ability to help her children continues on
from babyhood and manhood into maturity. Blessed is the son who
need not leave his mother at the threshold of the world's activities,
but may always and everywhere have her blessing and her help. Thrice
blessed are the son and the mother between whom there exists an association not only physical and affectional, but spiritual and intellectual,
and broad and wise as is the scope of each being.

LYDIA HOYT FARMER

Odysseus to Telemachus

My dear Telemachus,
The Trojan War
is over now; I don't recall who won it.
The Greeks, no doubt, for only they would leave
so many dead so far from their own homeland.

83

But still, my homeward way has proved too long.
While we were wasting time there, old Poseidon,
it almost seems, stretched and extended space.

I don't know where I am or what this place
can be. It would appear some filthy island,
with bushes, buildings, and great grunting pigs.
A garden choked with weeds; some queen or other.
Grass and huge stones . . . Telemachus, my son!
To a wanderer the faces of all islands
resemble one another. And the mind
trips, numbering waves; eyes, sore from sea horizons,
run; and the flesh of water stuffs the ears.
I can't remember how the war came out;
even how old you are—I can't remember.

Grow up, then, my Telemachus, grow strong.
Only the gods know if we'll see each other
again. You've long since ceased to be that babe
before whom I reined in the plowing bullocks.
Had it not been for Palamedes' trick
we two would still be living in one household.
But maybe he was right; away from me
you are quite safe from all Oedipal passions,
and your dreams, my Telemachus, are blameless.

JOSEPH BRODSKY

Did I Do Something Wrong?

Quality time and vitamin C and a book before bedtime at night,
I did everything right.
Then why, when I reach out to touch him, does he hold me at bay?
Something inside of me dies
When I look in my son's shuttered eyes,
So far from here. So very far away.

Tricking and treating and soccer games and the second grade's
    Halloween show,
I was sure to go.
And yet he is stumbling through jungles of bitterest black,
Lost in the fog that he buys,
Wearing a rebel's disguise,
Unwilling, or unable, to come back.

    I never claimed to be the perfect mother.
    I made mistakes. Well, everybody did.
    But God, I was so glad to be his mother.
    And God, oh God, oh God, I loved this kid.
    I love this kid.

Patience and laughter and trips to the beach and tickles and song,
Did I do something wrong?
Am I kidding myself? Am I simply rewriting the poem?

Telling myself a few lies,
While somewhere a frightened child cries,
And I wait, and I hope, and I pray that he'll find his way home.

JUDITH VIORST

Boundary Man

You are sixteen, male.
Tufts of new dark hair
announce themselves daily.
Sometimes I can't help myself.
I reach out to touch your face.

No touching, you warn
in your deepest tenor.
You are half-serious, half-teasing,
I pull back my hand,
awed by your authority.
My son, the boundary man.

I whine a little,
preparing to negotiate.
How about a little hug?

Mother, No. I'm untouchable.
Your smile seeps through.
You're goofy and dead serious
at the same time.
You know that you're right.

It's no secret to either of us
that I want to cuddle you again
and it's too late.

I remember when the top of your head
felt like silk,
and I couldn't stop kissing it.
I remember how pink and smooth
your cheeks were, warm
no matter what the weather.
I told you every day
You have the softest skin in the world.

And when you were 4 or 5,
I would hold you in my arms,
you facing backwards and
looking over my shoulder.
Sometimes you'd catch your father's eye
and stick out your tongue
and he'd laugh, both of you

knowing exactly what you didn't need to say:
Ha-ha. I've got her now.

It was fine with me to be wanted like that,
fought over as you enacted this age-old battle,
I was never in a rush to let you go.

And now, I can't help staring
at your face as it fills,
day by day, with those hairs
from the black lagoon.

I ask you too many times
if you are going to shave
or let it come in,
not caring at all
which choice you make.

You allow this conversation with me
about the destiny of your first beard hairs,
your voice low and gentle,
letting me back in for a moment
as you contemplate your manhood.

BARBARA KENNARD

She Pops Home

She pops home just long enough
    to overload the washing machine
    to spend a couple of hours on the phone
    to spray the bathroom mirror with lacquer
    to kick the stair-carpet out of line
    to say "that's new—can I borrow it?"
She pops home just long enough
    to dust the aspidistra with her elbow
    to squeak her hand down the bannister
    to use the last of the toilet roll
    to leave her bite in the last apple
She pops home just long enough
    to raid her mother's drawer for tights
    to stock up with next month's pill
    to hug a tenner out of Dad
She pops home just long enough
    to horrify them with her irresponsibility
    to leave them sweating till next time
She pops home just long enough
    to light their pond like a kingfisher
She pops home just long enough

CAL CLOTHIER

A Little Tooth

Your baby grows a tooth, then two,
and four, and five, then she wants some meat
directly from the bone. It's all

over: she'll learn some words, she'll fall
in love with cretins, dolts, a sweet
talker on his way to jail. And you,

your wife, get old, flyblown, and rue
nothing. You did, you loved, your feet
are sore. It's dusk. Your daughter's tall.

THOMAS LUX

Passage

Momma, dearest to my sister-
hood, and door
upon which I lean my ear,
listen for whispers,

I know of whom
you never speak,
your voice a dove's wing.
Momma, Momma,

how do I begin
to tell you
that I need
the chaos of my calm?

The storm outside
would never come,
nor cease to pound,
if the wind did not have its way—

push, pull, push, pull.
I need some kind
of randomness to my order.
Please allow me time

to bay at my lunatic moon;
my jaws ache for closure.
Momma, Momma,
I stand just outside your door,

clinging like milk
to the bottom of your glass.
Give me the absence
of your presence.

No seeds would form
if the May flowers never stopped
blooming long enough for the color
wash to leave their cheeky petals

and sneak out the red October door
with the hurried taffeta rustle
that a hem makes
as it catches on rough stones.

Momma, Momma, I know you
want to hold me. I feel the ache
in your arms, the whiff
of wind as I pull away.

Close your eyes before they come undone.
I can't take you with me this time;
as I learn to walk, to run,
I will fall. I must fall.

Momma, Momma,
I come running to you,
my mouth full of marbles—
round words which roll

beneath our feet—and we dance
in circles, our arms wide,
slip on glinting cats eyes,
reach for the space between us.

My dry face takes a cool slide
on your breast of green satin;
I look for the tears you hide
from me like eggs on Easter.

Momma, Momma,
let me swim in your lake of sleep,
make the sound of rain
on a tin roof, tiptoeing

over the rafters where I try
to force my lids closed
so I may re-enter the dream
where I saw you once—

like dust in the sun, the static
pulls me into the place where the deepest
bruises find their darkest blue
before they turn black.

TRISH LINDSEY JAGGERS

Eclipse

This strange dusk at noon, masking
a fire that can sear our vision
with its intensity, the radio warning us
to shield our eyes.
It is noon for you also,
my daughter, and darkness travels
across your fierce light.
I make a pin-hole for a few words;
"How are you?" I ask lightly,
as if I could journey through space,
as if I could touch that raw
flaming. I am your mother
but I cannot pull the moon
down from the sky.

MARGUERITE GUZMAN BOUVARD

It kills you to see them grow up. But I guess it would kill you quicker
if they didn't.

BARBARA KINGSOLVER

Son of a Bitch

he slipped away
as smoothly
as he had slipped from my womb
when he had shot out
slick and flailing
small fists
cocked defiantly
at a world into
which he had
reluctantly
come

they never told me
to stop pushing
so by fourteen
he was completely
out of sight

GARRIE KEYMAN

My child, never forget the things I have taught you. Store my commands in your heart.

PROVERBS 3:1

The City of Myself

O sudden and impalpable faun, lost in the thickets of myself, I will hunt you down until you cease to haunt my eyes with hunger. I heard your foot-falls in the desert, I saw your shadow in old buried cities, I heard your laughter running down a million streets, but I did not find you there. And no leaf hangs for me in the forest; I shall lift no stone upon the hills; I shall find no door in any city. But in the city of myself, upon the continent of my soul, I shall find the forgotten language, the lost world, a door where I may enter, and music strange as any ever sounded; I shall haunt you, ghost, along the labyrinthine ways until—until?

THOMAS WOLFE

We want you to know that your humanity is good;
Your bodies are meant to be sources of comfort and joy.

We call upon you to use your knowledge with integrity,
To choose your path in life and relationships with care,
Respecting your own dignity and the dignity of others,
Acting from a center of compassion and truth.

You should know better than to ever exploit other people;
You should know better than to degrade or cheapen sexuality in your
    attitudes;
You should know better than to bring unwanted children into the world;
You should know better than to make yourselves or others sick.

We hope you will know the deep human joys of enduring love and
   intimacy;
We hope you will know yourselves as valued and valuable people;
We hope you will know the world as a place of fulfillment and delight.

KENDYL GIBBONS

Hand-Shadows
for a daughter, eighteen

Dear child, first-born, what I could give outright
I've given—now there is only a father's wishing.
What can I hang around your neck for magic,
or smuggle in your pocket? I would draw
you a contour map of the territory ahead
but in truth it could only show you X—you are here.
The rest would be your Terra Incognita.

Years ago, in the trees beside a mountain lake
after bedtime, your mother and I sat up
together, reading the fire. Each flame, leaping,
seemed a stroke of the future, a signal for us
for you asleep in your nest at the rim of firelight
where great jagged shadows danced like knives.
We faced our ignorance until the fire was ash.

Once, in the first transports of adolescence,
you wandered over the hills behind the Sky Ranch,
remember? Suddenly beyond your feet
the country plunged away to utter strangeness,
and you were lost. The south wind carried your cries
like birdsong. At last I found you quiet on a stone,
your eyes full of the world we do not own.

Now it is all before you—wonderful
beyond a father's bedtime reckoning,
beyond his fears. What is it love must say?
Go forth to the fullness of your being: may
a merry kindness look you in the face.
Where home was, may your travels bring
you to a fellowship of open hearts.

So love must change our parts, my child no longer
child. I stand rehearsing at the door,
and think how once at bedtime, a dozen years
ago, I taught you how to cross your wrists
in the bright lamp-light, and link your thumbs, so,
and there on the wall a great bird arose
and soared on shadow wings, to the wonderment of all.

JAROLD RAMSEY

Any Man's Advice to His Son

If you have lost the radio beam, then guide yourself by the sun or the stars.

(By the North Star at night, and in daytime by the compass and the sun.)

Should the sky be overcast and there are neither stars nor a sun, then steer by dead reckoning.

If the wind and direction and speed are not known, then trust to your wits and your luck.

Do you follow me? Do you understand? Or is this too difficult to learn?

But you must and you will, it is important that you do,

Because there may be troubles even greater than these that I have said.

Because, remember this: Trust no man fully.

Remember: If you must shoot at another man squeeze, do not jerk the trigger.

Otherwise you may miss and die, yourself, at the hand of some other man's son.

And remember: In all this world there is nothing so easily squandered, or once gone,

so completely lost as life.

I tell you this because I remember you when you were small,

And because I remember all your monstrous infant boasts and lies,

And the way you smiled, and how you ran and climbed, as no one
    else quite did, and how you fell and were bruised,
And because there is no other person, anywhere on earth, who
    remembers these things as clearly as I do now.

KENNETH FEARING

This is what you shall do: Love the earth and sun and the animals,
despise riches, give alms to every one that asks, stand up for the stupid
and crazy, devote your income and labor to others, hate tyrants, argue
not concerning God, have patience and indulgence toward the people,
take off your hat to nothing known or unknown, or to any man or
number of men—go freely with powerful uneducated persons, and
with the young, and with the mothers of families—re-examine all you
have been told in school or church or in any book, and dismiss whatever insults your own soul; and your very flesh shall be a great poem,
and have the richest fluency, not only in its words, but in the silent lines
of its lips and face, and between the lashes of your eyes, and in every
motion and joint of your body.

WALT WHITMAN

Map of the Journey in Progress

Here is where I found my voice and chose to be brave.

Here's a place where I forgave someone, against my better judgment, and I survived that, and unexpectedly, amazingly, I became wiser.

Here's where I was once forgiven, was ready for once in my life to receive forgiveness and to be transformed. And I survived that also. I lived to tell the tale.

This is the place where I said no, more loudly than I'd thought I ever could, and everybody stared, but I said no loudly anyway, because I knew it must be said, and those staring settled down into harmless, ineffective grumbling, and over me they had no power anymore.

Here's a time, and here's another, when I laid down my fear and walked right on into it, right up to my neck into that roiling water.

Here's where cruelty taught me something. And here's where I was first astonished by gratuitous compassion and knew it for the miracle it was, the requirement it is. It was a trembling time.

And here, much later, is where I returned the blessing, clumsily. It wasn't hard, but I was unaccustomed. It cycled round, and as best I could I sent it back on out, passed the gift along. This circular motion, around and around, has no apparent end.

Here's a place, a murky puddle, where I have stumbled more than once and fallen. I don't know yet what to learn there.

On this site I was outraged and the rage sustains me still; it clarifies my seeing.

And here's where something caught me—a warm breeze in late winter, birdsong in late summer.

Here's where I was told that something was wrong with my eyes, that I see the world strangely, and here's where I said, "Yes, I know, I walk in beauty."

Here is where I began to look with my own eyes and listen with my ears and sing my own song, shaky as it is.

Here is where, as if by surgeon's knife, my heart was opened up—and here, and here, and here, and here. These are the landmarks of conversion.

VICTORIA SAFFORD

Do not be too timid and squeamish about your actions. All life is an experiment. The more experiments you make the better. What if they are a little coarse, and you may get your coat soiled or torn? What if you do fail, and get fairly rolled in the dirt once or twice? Up again, you shall never be so afraid of a tumble.

RALPH WALDO EMERSON

None of us can provide all the answers you will need as your life unfolds.

We know that the greatest joys and highest satisfactions are given to those who are faithful to their ideals, their promises, and their friends.

It does not matter if the world looks with disdain or suspicion upon the gifts you bring: give them anyway.

In the end, you must answer to your own conscience.

Trust yourself, and strive to be worthy of trust.

Remember all that lives must die, and do not fear to love, but embrace grief when it comes to you.

You will never know everything; but in the persistent desire to learn more, wisdom will grow.

To do what you know is wrong, or to cause pain needlessly, will always damage yourself in the long run.

The more you look for the best in others, the more you will find it.

Be of good courage, willingly do your share of the world's work, and remember that you are greatly loved.

KENDYL GIBBONS

My son, be attentive to my words; incline your ear to my sayings.
Let them not escape from your sight; keep them within your heart.
For they are life to him who finds them, and healing to all his flesh.
Keep your heart with all vigilance; for from it flow the springs of life.
Put away from you crooked speech, and put devious talk far from you.
Let your eyes look directly forward, and your gaze be straight before you.
Take heed to the path of your feet, then all your ways will be sure.
Do not swerve to the right or to the left; turn your foot away from evil.

PROVERBS 4:20–27

A World to Make

Bedeck your living with good hours
As with a garland of bright flowers.
With ornaments of truth and right
Make your mind's countenance more bright.
With knowledge and humility,
Engrave your face with dignity;
With loving make your heart more pure;
With justice make your hand more sure.

KENNETH L. PATTON

The Pomegranate

The only legend I have ever loved is
the story of a daughter lost in hell.
And found and rescued there.
Love and blackmail are the gist of it.
Ceres and Persephone the names.
And the best thing about the legend is
I can enter it anywhere. And have.
As a child in exile in
a city of fogs and strange consonants,
I read it first and at first I was
an exiled child in the crackling dusk of
the underworld, the stars blighted. Later
I walked out in a summer twilight
searching for my daughter at bed-time.
When she came running I was ready
to make any bargain to keep her.
I carried her back past whitebeams
and wasps and honey-scented buddleias.
But I was Ceres then and I knew
winter was in store for every leaf
on every tree on that road.
Was inescapable for each one we passed.
And for me.
             It is winter
and the stars are hidden.

I climb the stairs and stand where I can see
my child asleep beside her teen magazines,
her can of Coke, her plate of uncut fruit.
The pomegranate! How did I forget it?
She could have come home and been safe
and ended the story and all
our heart-broken searching but she reached
out a hand and plucked a pomegranate.
She put out her hand and pulled down
the French sound for apple and
the noise of stone and the proof
that even in the place of death,
at the heart of legend, in the midst
of rocks full of unshed tears
ready to be diamonds by the time
the story was told, a child can be
hungry. I could warn her. There is still a chance.
The rain is cold. The road is flint-coloured.
The suburb has cars and cable television.
The veiled stars are above ground.
It is another world. But what else
can a mother give her daughter but such
beautiful rifts in time?
If I defer the grief I will diminish the gift.
The legend will be hers as well as mine.
She will enter it. As I have.

She will wake up. She will hold
the papery flushed skin in her hand.
And to her lips. I will say nothing.

For this is the journey that men make, to find themselves. If they fail in
this, it doesn't matter much what else they find. Money, fame, position,
many loves, revenge—all are of little consequence. And when the tickets
are collected at the end of the ride they are tossed into a bin marked
failure. But if a man happens to find himself—if he knows what he can
be depended upon to do, the limits of his courage, the position from
which he will no longer retreat, the degree to which he can surrender
his inner life to some woman, the secret reservoirs of his determination,
the extent of his dedication, the depth of his feeling for beauty, his honest
and unpostured goals—then he has found a mansion which he can
inhabit with dignity all the days of his life.

JAMES MICHENER

My best advice for Black college students, and all students, is to focus
on making a life rather than just a living. Remember the key priorities
the elders and mentors in our community have always embraced:

dedication to excellence, faith in God, respect for yourself and others around you, the value of hard work, the importance of education, and a commitment of service to others as the rent we all pay for living. Focus on finding your purpose and the job God has placed you in the world to do. Stand for something bigger than yourself. Repay the opportunities you have been given as you go forward by reaching back for someone else's hand.

MARIAN WRIGHT EDELMAN

Stand in the company of the elders. Who is wise? Attach yourself to
    such a one.
Be ready to listen to every godly discourse, and let no wise proverbs
    escape you.
If you see an intelligent person, rise early to visit him; let your foot
    wear out his doorstep.

ECCLESIASTICUS 6:34–36

Read myths. They teach you that you can turn inward, and you begin to get the message of the symbols. Read other people's myths, not those of your own religion, because you tend to interpret your own religion in terms of facts—but if you read the other ones, you begin to get the message. Myth helps you to put your mind in touch with this experience of being alive. It tells you what the experience is.

JOSEPH CAMPBELL

In the final analysis, the key to my immortality, the reassurance that my life has mattered and was not lived in vain, is not that different from the key to yours or anyone else's. I find it in the work I have done, the acts of kindness I have performed, the love I have given and the love I have received, the people who will smile when they remember me, and the children and grandchildren through whom my name and memory will be perpetuated.

HAROLD S. KUSHNER

Will you seek afar off? you surely come back at last,
In things best known to you, finding the best, or as good as the best,
In folks nearest to you finding the sweetest, strongest, lovingest;
Happiness, knowledge, not in another place, but this place—not for
    another hour, but this hour.

WALT WHITMAN

The Way

I must live my own way,
Refusing all that binds.
I must know my own mind
Among all other minds.
I must do my own deeds,
And in whatever lands.
I will know my own hands
Among all other hands.

I must forsake the crowds,
And walk with lonely fools,
To seek for my own face
In bleak, deserted pools.
I must leave worn old roads,
To walk on hillside grass,
To follow my own feet
Out in the wilderness.

KENNETH L. PATTON

This is what youth must figure out:
Girls, love, and living.
The having, the not having,
The spending and giving,
And the melancholy time of not knowing.

E. B. WHITE

My grandmother walked over and put her hand on my shoulder.

"Listen. Listen before it passes. *Paròl gin pié zèl.* The words can give wings to your feet. There is so much to say, but time has failed you," she said. "There is a place where women are buried in clothes the color of flames, where we drop coffee on the ground for those who went ahead, where the daughter is never fully a woman until her mother has passed on before her. There is always a place where, if you listen closely in the night, you will hear your mother telling a story and at the end of the tale, she will ask you this question: *'Ou libéré?'* Are you free, my daughter?"

My grandmother quickly pressed her fingers over my lips.

"Now," she said, "you will know how to answer."

EDWIDGE DANTICAT

Happy are those who find wisdom, and those who get understanding,
for her income is better than silver, and her revenue better than gold.
She is more precious than jewels, and nothing you desire can compare
with her.
Long life is in her right hand; in her left hand are riches and honor.
Her ways are ways of pleasantness, and all her paths are peace.
She is a tree of life to those who lay hold of her; those who hold her
fast are called happy.

PROVERBS 3:13–18

If—

If you can keep your head when all about you
    Are losing theirs and blaming it on you;
If you can trust yourself when all men doubt you,
    But make allowance for their doubting too;
If you can wait and not be tired by waiting,
    Or, being lied about, don't deal in lies,
Or, being hated, don't give way to hating,
    And yet don't look too good, nor talk too wise;

If you can dream—and not make dreams your master;
    If you can think—and not make thoughts your aim;
If you can meet with triumph and disaster
    And treat those two imposters just the same;

If you can bear to hear the truth you've spoken
    Twisted by knaves to make a trap for fools,
Or watch the things you gave your life to broken,
    And stoop and build 'em up with wornout tools;

If you can make one heap of all your winnings
    And risk it on one turn of pitch-and-toss,
And lose, and start again at your beginnings
    And never breathe a word about your loss;
If you can force your heart and nerve and sinew
    To serve your turn long after they are gone,
And so hold on when there is nothing in you
    Except the Will which says to them: "Hold on";

If you can talk with crowds and keep your virtue,
    Or walk with kings—nor lose the common touch;
If neither foes nor loving friends can hurt you;
    If all men count with you, but none too much;
If you can fill the unforgiving minute
    With sixty seconds' worth of distance run—
Yours is the Earth and everything that's in it,
    And—which is more—you'll be a Man, my son!

RUDYARD KIPLING

But there comes a moment, somewhere in adolescence, when we know that we must go out, cross our Red Sea, and establish our independence. Ah, freedom! How we long for it. But then, like the children of Israel, we discover that freedom is a desert, a place to get lost. We wander about; we wish we were back amid the "flesh pots of Egypt." But somehow we search on until we discover a holy mountain where there is a Law of Life, some rules to live by. We try them out. Sometimes we disobey to see what will happen, and we suffer. We go astray and find our way back. Finally, after forty years of discovery, clarification, discipline, and self-discipline, we see the river, the Jordan River, shining in the distance, and the Promised Land just over there ahead. But then we, like Moses, are told that we aren't going across. We've found our way, but those who come after us will inherit the land, and maybe think of us and thank us for our having shown the way. And then suddenly, we may realize that the meaning was somehow in the pilgrimage itself, and all that it required of us, and what we all experienced along the way.

DONALD S. HARRINGTON

Be as Frodo

Be as Frodo.
Never take for granted all the comforts of the Shire.
Respect your Elders and care for them.
Know the worth of close friends.

Be as Frodo.
Have a pure heart.
Accept adventure as it comes.
Make new friends.

Be as Frodo.
See the good in others.
Love the unlovable.
Trust your instincts.

Be as Frodo.
Know your path.
Though the way is long and hard, persevere.
Accept the help of friends.

Be as Frodo.
Be unselfish.
Work for the good.
Be a good friend.

Be as Frodo.
Know that you may have to go on alone.
When there is no hope, believe in yourself.
Fight against evil.

Be as Frodo.
And failing that,
Be as Sam.

MELINDA M. PERRIN

Daughter of love, sister of truth, may you go with courage upon the
    path of life that lies before you.
Keep a pure heart, a free mind, a steadfast will, and a joyous song for
    the journey.
May you be simple in your desires, loyal in your friendships, and
    strong in all tribulation.
Be proud of your womanhood, and serve the highest good you find
    with your whole devotion.
May life reward you with fruitful happiness,
and may you never forget the ideals to which you have pledged yourself
    today,
and the fullness of love by which you are here surrounded and
    blessed.

KENDYL GIBBONS

The Road Not Taken

Two roads diverged in a yellow wood,
And sorry I could not travel both
And be one traveler, long I stood
And looked down one as far as I could
To where it bent in the undergrowth;

Then took the other, as just as fair,
And having perhaps the better claim,
Because it was grassy and wanted wear;
Though as for that, the passing there
Had worn them really about the same,

And both that morning equally lay
In leaves no step had trodden black.
Oh, I kept the first for another day!
Yet knowing how way leads on to way,
I doubted if I should ever come back.

I shall be telling this with a sigh
Somewhere ages and ages hence:
Two roads diverged in a wood, and I—
I took the one less traveled by,
And that has made all the difference.

ROBERT FROST

And heed the counsel of your own heart, for no one is more faithful
to you than it is.
For our own mind sometimes keeps us better informed than seven
sentinels sitting high on a watchtower.

ECCLESIASTICUS 37:13–14

True Teachers

Rest never your travels until you can find
The man who has learned how to love with his mind,
And search till you find him, and spare no expense,
The man who has passion that lives upon sense.

Leave off your fine learning until you can sit
With teachers whose pity is salted with wit.
Succumb not to weeping until you have sought
The man whose own sorrowing cries with his thought.

Then seek and seek further until you attain
The man who has wonder alive in his brain.
Count no man your ally until he can sight
The stars of the daytime, the sun of the night.

KENNETH L. PATTON

Growing up is the hardest thing we'll ever do. And it really is all we ever do. We move through each stage—learning all we can, then figuring out what's important and what can be left behind. We look for counsel, we resist advice, we acquire everything we think is important and load our baggage, and then we struggle trying to carry backpacks too heavy. We unload, we go on, and maybe later we find out that what we left was what we needed and what we brought is not helpful. And so we start again. Learning, acquiring, sorting through the packing, leaving stuff behind, choosing pathways, feeling bound, feeling alone, feeling crowded in.

As each of us grows—through childhood to adolescence to adulthood, through stages of discovery and mastery of each stage of our lives—we encounter the challenges of casting off clothes which no longer fit us, of knowing ourselves anew, of feeling our own worth, and of finding what freedom really means.

And it seems to me that we go through it over and over—the journey is not a single continuous path. We continually repeat the cycle of feeling free, becoming encumbered, striving to understand and to learn more, then freeing ourselves again, until finally we can know ourselves, become ourselves.

LINDA OLSON PEEBLES

Now I Become Myself

Now I become myself. It's taken
Time, many years and places;
I have been dissolved and shaken,
Worn other people's faces,
Run madly, as if Time were there,
Terribly old, crying a warning,
"Hurry, you will be dead before—"
(What? Before you reach the morning?
Or the end of the poem is clear?
Or love safe in the walled city?)
Now to stand still, to be here,
Feel my own weight and density!
The black shadow on the paper
Is my hand; the shadow of a word
As thought shapes the shaper
Falls heavy on the page, is heard.
All fuses now, falls into place
From wish to action, word to silence,
My work, my love, my time, my face
Gathered into one intense
Gesture of growing like a plant.
As slowly as the ripening fruit
Fertile, detached, and always spent,
Falls but does not exhaust the root,
So all the poem is, can give,

Grows in me to become the song,
Made so and rooted so by love.
Now there is time and Time is young.
O, in this single hour I live
All of myself and do not move.
I, the pursued, who madly ran,
Stand still, stand still, and stop the sun!

MAY SARTON

We have not even to risk the adventure alone, for the heroes of all time have gone before us. The labyrinth is thoroughly known. We have only to follow the thread of the hero path, and where we had thought to find an abomination, we shall find a god. And where we had thought to slay another, we shall slay ourselves. Where we had thought to travel outward, we will come to the center of our own existence. And where we had thought to be alone, we will be with all the world.

JOSEPH CAMPBELL

Wisdom

When I have ceased to break my wings
Against the faultiness of things,
And learned that compromises wait
Behind each hardly opened gate,
When I can look Life in the eyes,
Grown calm and very coldly wise,
Life will have given me the Truth,
And taken in exchange—my youth.

SARA TEASDALE

Reflect, then, my young friend, seriously and prayerfully, on the importance of the season through which you are now passing. Little do you think how deep an interest is felt for your welfare. There is the man that begat you, and the woman that bare you, each crying out, "My son, if thy heart shall be wise, my heart shall rejoice, even mine." Kind friends draw near and ask for blessings on your heads, which shall reach to the utmost bounds of the everlasting hills. Your minister prays that you may become his joy and the crown of his rejoicing in the day of the Lord Jesus. Above all, God himself looks down, and blending his claims with your highest welfare, speaks out, "My son, give me thy heart." Oh, shall all this interest be felt for you, in heaven and on earth, in vain! Will you not at this early hour on the dial of human life, realize the grandeur and glory of the destiny that awaits you!

Be faithful to yourselves, to your fellow-men, and to God for ten, fifteen, or twenty years, and I almost dare promise you a useful life, a happy death, and a blissful immortality.

DAVID MAGIE

First Lesson

Lie back, daughter, let your head
be tipped back in the cup of my hand.
Gently, and I will hold you. Spread
your arms wide, lie out on the stream
and look high at the gulls. A dead-
man's-float is face down. You will dive
and swim soon enough where this tidewater
ebbs to the sea. Daughter, believe
me, when you tire on the long thrash
to your island, lie up, and survive.
As you float now, where I held you
and let go, remember when fear
cramps your heart what I told you:
lie gently and wide to the light-year
stars, lie back, and the sea will hold you.

PHILIP BOOTH

Ithaka

As you set out for Ithaka
hope the voyage is a long one,
full of adventure, full of discovery,
Laistrygonians and Cyclops,
angry Poseidon—don't be afraid of them:
you'll never find things like that on your way
as long as you keep your thoughts raised high,
as long as a rare excitement
stirs your spirit and your body.
Laistrygonians and Cyclops,
wild Poseidon—you won't encounter them
unless you bring them along inside your soul,
unless your soul sets them up in front of you.
Hope the voyage is a long one.
May there be many a summer morning when,
with what pleasure, what joy,
you come into harbors seen for the first time;
may you stop at Phoenician trading stations
to buy fine things,
mother of pearl and coral, amber and ebony,
sensual perfume of every kind—
as many sensual perfumes as you can;
and may you visit many Egyptian cities
to gather stores of knowledge from their scholars.

Keep Ithaka always in your mind.
Arriving there is what you are destined for.
But do not hurry the journey at all.
Better if it lasts for years,
so you are old by the time you reach the island,
wealthy with all you have gained on the way,
not expecting Ithaka to make you rich.

Ithaka gave you the marvelous journey.
Without her you would not have set out.
She has nothing left to give you now.
And if you find her poor, Ithaka won't have fooled you.
Wise as you will have become, so full of experience,
you will have understood by then what these Ithakas mean.

C. P. CAVAFY

A Passionate Light

In Youth I Have Known One

In youth I have known one with whom the Earth
In secret communing held—as he with it,
In daylight, and in beauty, from his birth:
Whose fervid, flickering torch of life was lit
From the sun and stars, whence he had drawn forth
A passionate light—such for his spirit was fit—
And yet that spirit knew—not in the hour
Of its own fervour—what had o'er it power.

EDGAR ALLAN POE

When the Big Blue Light Comes a Whirling Up Behind

Leaning back in the white vinyl of your rear-high
Mustang, forest green shining in as big a Saturday sun
as any June day could find,
perfect for opening her out down to the beach
when the big blue light comes a whirling up behind

and pulls you over. The trooper
fills your window. What's the rush, kid?
Let's see your license if you have one.

You fumble it out. Your fingers ache. He lumbers
back to his car, sits under the whirling light
and writes while traffic goes by like planes.
How much is there to write?
Here he comes.

He hands you the ticket and license.
Save your hotshot stuff for the amusement park.
Kid, you drive like that again
you'll never drive again.

He swings out into traffic. You wait
and you wait longer.
Then you start her up,
signal, look,
pull out and stick in the right lane.

Your speedometer won't stay steady.
You try to breathe all the way through yourself.
You would like to tell him
where he can go shine his leather.
You would like a button on your dash
that says WINGS.

PETER SEARS

Grasping at Ghosts

She lights a stub of candle,
studies its slow burn and dissolve
into a brass bowl.
I watch her from the edge
of the kitchen.

It was the crackling that woke us,
roar of heat devouring cedar.
I took her from her crib, fled
down darkened stairs, out
to cool lawn, cold moon.

Eleven now, her fingertips dart
through fire, some unspoken
rite of passage I learned
from my grandmother,
entrusted now to my daughter.

Glass shattered as sirens
whined past, unable to find us.
Now open, our house
sucked fire into its body,
a phoenix igniting.

She tips the candle,
drips wax onto a napkin,
squeezes it between long fingers.
Her red hair flickers in the spit of light
as she shapes the cooling flesh.

From ash we built again,
exhumed bones and sooty reek,
broken teeth of window, rusted nail—
secrets of past fires rising
to the surface.

I stand in the kitchen a while longer
before telling her *Enough is enough.*
She sighs,
blows out the tiny flare,
grasping at the trail of passing ghosts.

RONDA BROATCH

The male is not less the soul, nor more—he too is in his place;
He too is all qualities—he is action and power;
The flush of the known universe is in him;
Scorn becomes him well, and appetite and defiance become him well;
The wildest largest passions, bliss that is utmost, sorrow that is utmost,

become him well—pride is for him;
The full-spread pride of man is calming and excellent to the soul;
Knowledge becomes him—he likes it always—he brings everything
    to the test of himself;
Whatever the survey, whatever the sea and the sail, he strikes soundings
    at last only here;
(Where else does he strike soundings, except here?)

WALT WHITMAN

Beautiful are the youth
whose rich emotions flash and burn,
whose lithe bodies filled with energy and grace
sway in their happy dance of life

ROBERT T. WESTON

Caught Before Flight

Sun is sparkling on top of blue water
A summer thunderstorm is moving in
I still have that picture tucked inside a dusty red photo album
I stand with my father on the dock in front of a dark lake
Behind us the people of summer drift in their boats

He holds my waist as we pose
His straight arm keeping a distance between us
I tilt my head away from him
I let the breeze play with my hair
My hands
Two white doves before flight
Are caught in front of my waist

He wears faded jeans and oil-stained boat shoes
I go barefoot in denim cutoffs
New breasts molded into a ruffled tube top
My father's face is captured in a stiff grin
He can no longer cover me up
With guilt
With clothing
With his eyes
This is my summer of love
He is my chauffeur

Over his left shoulder
Two teenage boys in a white and red speed boat
Grin like wolves at my abundance
The pastel flowers on my top fade into my tan skin
Clouds in the blue sky frame our heads
I look into the camera's eye and smile
Summer begins

Days spent skinny-dipping with boys in secret coves
Water running off our bodies shiny as minnows
As we pull ourselves into boats
To make out in the silent heat of the afternoons

Nights filled with stars pasted into the distant sky
Beer kisses from a dark-haired boy in the back of a boat
Rocked by the oily water and our struggles
A blond-haired boy's desperate fingers in my bikini
As my father snores in our cabin under the trees

The storm hits late the third of July
Heat lightning first
Torrential rain by morning
Leaves drop into the lake with the weight of the wind
Father and I leave in the dark with the car's heater at full blast
We race in silence
Down slick back roads towards home
We race
As if with so much speed
He could leave behind
What I had found

VICKI WHICKER

On the Road to Womanhood

Be free to be you
Be strong, yet gentle,
Be proud, yet loving.
May your body always be
A blessing to you,
A sacred grove of love and pleasure.
So care for your body
As you would for a beautiful garden.
Your womb can now bring forth new life
But remember yours is the power
To open or close the gates of life
In your garden.
Therefore yours is the responsibility
To be a conscious gardener.
Open to the embrace of love
When you find the one
Who is truly deserving.

KSENIJA SOSTER-OLMER

Young men, in the conduct and manage of actions, embrace more than they can hold; stir more than they can quiet; fly to the end, without consideration of the means and degrees; pursue some few principles which they have chanced upon absurdly; care not to innovate, which draws unknown inconveniences; use extreme remedies at first; and that which doubleth all errors will not acknowledge or retract them; like an unready horse, that will neither stop nor turn.

FRANCIS BACON

The Discovery of Sex

We try to be discreet standing in the dark
hallway by the front door. He gets his hands
up inside the front of my shirt and I put mine
down inside the back of his jeans. We are crazy
for skin, each other's skin, warm silky skin.
Our tongues are in each other's mouths,
where they belong, home at last. At first

we hope my mother won't see us, but later we don't care,
we forget her. Suddenly she makes a noise
like a game show alarm and says Hey! Stop that!
and we put our hands out where she can see them.
Our mouths stay pressed together, though, and
when she isn't looking anymore our hands go
back inside each other's clothes. We could

go where no one can see us, but we are
good kids, from good families, trying to have

as much discreet sex as possible with my mother and father
four feet away watching strangers kiss on TV,
my mother and father who once did as we are doing,
something we can't imagine because we know

that before we put our mouths together, before
the back seat of his parents' car where our skins
finally become one—before us, these things
were unknown! Our parents look on in disbelief
as we pioneer delights they thought only they knew
before those delights gave them us.

Years later, still we try to be discreet, standing
in the kitchen now where we think she can't see us. I
slip my hands down inside the back of his jeans
and he gets up under the front of my shirt.
We open our mouths to kiss and suddenly Hey! Hey!
says our daughter glaring from the kitchen doorway.
Get a room! she says, as we put our hands
out where she can see them.

DEBRA SPENCER

poem in praise of menstruation

if there is a river
more beautiful than this
bright as the blood
red edge of the moon if
there is a river
more faithful than this
returning each month
to the same delta if there

is a river
braver than this
coming and coming in a surge
of passion, of pain if there is

a river
more ancient than this
daughter of eve
mother of cain and of abel if there is in

the universe such a river if
there is some where water
more powerful than this wild
water

pray that it flows also
through animals
beautiful and faithful and ancient
and female and brave

LUCILLE CLIFTON

I sing the Body electric;
The armies of those I love engirth me, and I engirth them;
They will not let me off till I go with them, respond to them,
And discorrupt them, and charge them full with the charge of the Soul.

Was it doubted that those who corrupt their own bodies conceal
themselves;
And if those who defile the living are as bad as they who defile the dead?
And if the body does not do as much as the Soul?
And if the body were not the Soul, what is the Soul?

WALT WHITMAN

Adolescence I

In water-heavy nights behind grandmother's porch
We knelt in the tickling grass and whispered:
Linda's face hung before us, pale as a pecan,
And it grew wise as she said:
    "A boy's lips are soft,
    As soft as baby's skin."
The air closed over her words.
A firefly whirred in the air, and in the distance
I could hear streetlamps ping
Into miniature suns
Against a feathery sky.

RITA DOVE

Fifteen

South of the bridge on Seventeenth
I found back of the willows one summer
day a motorcycle with engine running
as it lay on its side, ticking over
slowly in the high grass. I was fifteen.

I admired all that pulsing gleam, the
shiny flanks, the demure headlights

fringed where it lay; I led it gently
to the road, and stood with that
companion, ready and friendly. I was fifteen.

We could find the end of a road, meet
the sky on out Seventeenth. I thought about
hills, and patting the handle got back a
confident opinion. On the bridge we indulged
a forward feeling, a tremble. I was fifteen.

Thinking, back farther in the grass I found
the owner, just coming to, where he had flipped
over the rail. He had blood on his hand, was pale—
I helped him walk to his machine. He ran his hand
over it, called me good man, roared away.

I stood there, fifteen.

WILLIAM STAFFORD

I went to the woods because I wished to live deliberately, to front
only the essential facts of life, and see if I could not learn what it had
to teach, and not, when I came to die, discover that I had not lived.
I did not wish to live what was not life, living is so dear; nor did I

wish to practise resignation, unless it was quite necessary. I wanted to live deep and suck out all the marrow of life, to live so sturdily and Spartan-like as to put to rout all that was not life, to cut a broad swath and shave close, to drive life into a corner, and reduce it to its lowest terms, and, if it proved to be mean, why then to get the whole and genuine meanness of it, and publish its meanness to the world; or if it were sublime, to know it by experience, and be able to give a true account of it in my next excursion.

HENRY DAVID THOREAU

So God has armed youth and puberty and manhood no less with its own piquancy and charm, and made it enviable and gracious and its claims not to be put by, if it will stand by itself. Do not think the youth has no force, because he cannot speak to you and me. Hark! in the next room his voice is sufficiently clear and emphatic. It seems he knows how to speak to his contemporaries. Bashful or bold then, he will know how to make us seniors very unnecessary.

The nonchalance of boys who are sure of a dinner, and would disdain as much as a lord to do or say aught to conciliate one, is the healthy attitude of human nature. A boy is in the parlor what the pit is in the playhouse; independent, irresponsible, looking out from his corner on such people and facts as pass by, he tries and sentences them on their merits, in the swift, summary way of boys, as good, bad, interesting, silly, eloquent, troublesome. He cumbers himself never about consequences, about interests; he gives an independent, genuine verdict. You must court him; he does not court you.

Ralph Waldo Emerson

What we are usually invited to contemplate as "ripeness" in a man is the resigning of ourselves to an almost exclusive use of the reason. One acquires it by copying others and getting rid, one by one, of the thoughts and convictions which were dear in the days of one's youth. We believed once in the victory of truth; but we do not now. We believed in goodness; we do not now. We were zealous for justice; but we are not so now. We trusted in the power of kindness and peace-ableness; we do not now. We were capable of enthusiasm; but we are not so now. To get through the shoals and storms of life more easily we have lightened our craft, throwing overboard what we thought could be spared. But it was really our stock of food and drink of which we deprived ourselves; our craft is now easier to manage, but we ourselves are in a decline.

I listened, in my youth, to conversations between grown-up people through which there breathed a tone of sorrowful regret which oppressed the heart. The speakers looked back at the idealism and capacity for enthusiasm of their youth as something precious to which they ought to have held fast, and yet at the same time they regarded it as almost a law of nature that no one should be able to do so. This woke in me a dread of having ever, even once, to look back on my own past with such a feeling; I resolved never to let myself become subject to this tragic domination of mere reason, and what I thus vowed in almost boyish defiance I have tried to carry out.

ALBERT SCHWEITZER

The Leaden-Eyed

Let not young souls be smothered out before
They do quaint deeds and fully flaunt their pride.
It is the world's one crime its babes grow dull,
Its poor are ox-like, limp and leaden-eyed.
Not that they starve; but starve so dreamlessly,
Not that they sow, but that they seldom reap.
Not that they serve, but have no gods to serve,
Not that they die, but that they die like sheep.

VACHEL LINDSAY

Our age is retrospective. It builds the sepulchres of the fathers. It writes biographies, histories, and criticism. The foregoing generations beheld God and nature face to face; we, through their eyes. Why should not we also enjoy an original relation to the universe? Why should not we have a poetry and philosophy of insight and not of tradition, and a religion by revelation to us, and not the history of theirs? Embosomed for a season in nature, whose floods of life stream around and through us, and invite us by the powers they supply, to action proportioned to nature, why should we grope among the dry bones of the past, or put the living generation into masquerade out of its faded wardrobe? The sun shines to-day also. There is more wool and flax in the fields. There are new lands, new men, new thoughts. Let us demand our own works and laws and worship.

RALPH WALDO EMERSON

It is not by wearing down into uniformity all that is individual in themselves, but by cultivating it and calling it forth, within the limits imposed by the rights and interests of others, that human beings become a noble and beautiful object of contemplation; and as the works partake the character of those who do them, by the same process human life also becomes rich, diversified, and animating, furnishing more abundant aliment to high thoughts and elevating feelings, and strengthening the tie which binds every individual to the race, by making the race infinitely better worth belonging to.

JOHN STUART MILL

The Secret

Two girls discover
the secret of life
in a sudden line of
poetry.

I who don't know the
secret wrote
the line. They
told me

(through a third person)
they had found it
but not what it was
not even

what line it was. No doubt
by now, more than a week
later, they have forgotten
the secret,

the line, the name of
the poem. I love them
for finding what
I can't find,

and for loving me
for the line I wrote,
and for forgetting it
so that

a thousand times, till death
finds them, they may
discover it again, in other
lines

in other
happenings. And for
wanting to know it,
for

assuming there is
such a secret, yes,
for that
most of all.

DENISE LEVERTOV

I believe the truth lies in youth; I believe it is always right against us. I believe that, far from trying to teach it, it is in youth that we, the elders, must seek our lessons. And I am well aware that youth is capable of errors; I know that our role is to forewarn youth as best we can: but I believe that often, when trying to protect youth, we impede it. I believe that each new generation arrives bearing a message that it must deliver; our role is to help that delivery. I believe that what is called "experience" is often but an unavowed fatigue, resignation, blighted hope.

There are very few of my contemporaries who have remained faithful to their youth. They have almost all compromised. That is what they call "learning from life." They have denied the truth that was in them. The borrowed truths are the ones to which one clings most tenaciously, and all the more so since they remain foreign to our intimate self. It takes much more precaution to deliver one's own message, much more boldness and prudence, than to sign up with and add one's voice to an already existing party.

ANDRÉ GIDE

If you have built castles in the air, your work need not be lost; that is where they should be. Now put the foundations under them.

HENRY DAVID THOREAU

I believe that my generation will see better things, too—that we will witness the time when AIDS is cured and cancer is defeated; when the Middle East will find peace and Africa grain, and the Cubs win the World Series—probably only once. I will see things as inconceivable to me today as a moon shot was to my grandfather when he was 16, or the Internet to my father when he was 16.

Ever since I was a little kid, whenever I've had a lousy day, my dad would put his arm around me and promise me that "tomorrow will be a better day." I challenged my father once, "How do you know that?" He said, "I just do." I believed him. My great-grandparents believed that, and my grandparents, and so do I.

JOSH RITTENBERG

We cannot always build the future for our youth, but we can build our youth for the future.

FRANKLIN D. ROOSEVELT

The Old Man Said: One

Some will tell
you it doesn't
matter. That is
a lie. Everything,
every single thing
matters. And
nothing good
happens fast.

CARROLL ARNETT

Index of First Lines

Credits

Selections appear on page numbers in bold.

APTER   *Altered Loves* (**10, 39**) by Terri Apter, 1990.

ACQUAFONDATA   "Marking Transitions" (**25**). Reprinted with permission of Lynn M. Acquafondata (Brodie).

ARISTOTLE   *Politics* (**26**) by Aristotle, 350 B.C.E.

ARNETT   "The Old Man Said: One" (**153**) by Carroll Arnett (Gogisgi), in *Night Perimeter: New and Selected Poems 1958-1990.* Copyright © 1979 by Carroll Arnett. Reprinted with permission of Greenfield Review Press.

BACON   "Of Youth and Age" (**138**), in *Essays, Civil and Moral* by Francis Bacon, 1914.

BALDWIN   *Notes of a Native Son* (**50**) by James Baldwin, 1955.

BASS   "First Menstruation" (**74**), in *Of Separateness and Merging* by Ellen Bass (New York: Autumn House/Random House, 1977). Copyright © 1977 by Ellen Bass. Reprinted with permission of author.

BELL   "Brief Reflection on Coming of Age as a Unitarian Universalist" (**12**), used with permission of Wendy L. Bell.

BLUME   *Are You There God? It's me, Margaret* (**39**) by Judy Blume, 1970.

BOLAND   "The Pomegranate" (**108**), in *A Time of Violence* by Eavan Boland. Copyright © 1994 by Eavan Boland. All rights reserved. Reprinted with permission of W. W. Norton & Company, Inc.

BOOTH   "First Lesson" (**126**) by Philip Booth, in *Letter from a Distant Land* by Philip Booth. Copyright © 1957 by Philip Booth. Reprinted with permission of Viking Penguin, a division of Penguin Group (USA) Inc.

BOUVARD   "Eclipse" (**94**) by Marguerite Guzman Bouvard, in *Literary Mama: Reading for the Maternally Inclined,* ed. Andrea J. Buchanan and Amy Hudock (Emeryville, Calif.: Seal Press, 2006). Reprinted with permission of author.

BRADLEY   *Yes, Your Teen Is Crazy! Loving Your Kid Without Losing Your Mind* (**37**) by Michael J. Bradley, 2002.

BREATHNACH   *Something More: Excavating Your Authentic Self* (**16**) by Sarah Ban Breathnach, 1998.

BROATCH   "Grasping at Ghosts" (**133**) by Ronda Broatch, in *Literary Mama: Reading for the Maternally Inclined,* ed. Andrea J. Buchanan and Amy Hudock (Emeryville, Calif.: Seal Press, 2006). Reprinted with permission of author.

BRODSKY   "Odysseus to Telemachus" (**83**), in *A Part of Speech* by Joseph Brodsky. Translation copyright © 1980 by Farrar, Straus & Giroux, Inc. Reprinted with permission of Farrar, Straus & Giroux, LLC.

BROOKHOUSE   "For Stephen" (**71**), in *The Light Between the Fields* by Christopher Brookhouse (Chapel Hill, North Carolina: Sigal Books, 1998). Copyright © 1998 by Christopher Brookhouse. Reprinted with permission of author.

BROWN   "Boyish Dreams of Manhood" (**60**) by Jennifer Brown. Reprinted with permission of author.

CAMPBELL   *The Power of Myth* (**111, 124**) by Joseph Campbell, 1988.

CAVAFY   "Ithaka" (**127**), in *Collected Poems of C. P. Cavafy*, Revised Edition, by C. P. Cavafy, translated by Edmund Keeley and Philip Sherrard. Copyright © 1972 by Edmund Keeley and Philip Sherrard. Reprinted with permission of Princeton University Press.

CHESS AND WHITBREAD   Selection (**50**) by Stella Chess and Jane Whitbread, in *The Columbia World of Quotations*, ed. Robert Andrews, Mary Biggs, and Michael Seidel, 1996.

CHURCH   "Who Am I?" (**26**). Reprinted with permission of Forrest Church.

CLIFTON   "poem in praise of menstruation" (**141**), in *Blessing the Boats: New and Selected Poems, 1988-2000* by Lucille Clifton. Copyright © 2000 by Lucille Clifton. Reprinted with permission of BOA Editions Ltd.

CLOTHIER   "She Pops Home" (**89**). Reprinted with permission of Cal Clothier.

COOLEY   Selection (**59**) by Mason Cooley, in *The Columbia World of Quotations*, ed. Robert Andrews, Mary Biggs, and Michael Seidel, 1996.

CROOKER   "My Middle Daughter, on the Edge of Adolescence, Learns to Play the Saxophone" (**35**), in *Psychological Perspectives*, 1990. Copyright © 1990 by Barbara Crooker. Reprinted with permission of author.

DANTICAT   *Breath, Eyes, Memory* (**114**) by Edwidge Danticat, 1994.

DE KONINCK   "Edge of the Nest" (**78**) by Jessica de Koninck, in *Literary Mama: Reading for the Maternally Inclined*, edited by Andrea J. Buchanan and Amy Hudock (Emeryville, Calif.: Seal Press, 2006). Reprinted with permission of author.

DECTER   "A Letter to the Young (and to Their Parents)" (**54**) by Midge Decter, in *The Atlantic Monthly*, February 1975.

DOE   *Nurturing Your Teenager's Soul* (**22**) by Mimi Doe, 2004.

DOVE   "Adolescence II" (**40**) and "Adolescence I" (**143**), in *Yellow House on the Corner* by Rita Dove (Pittsburgh: Carnegie-Mellon University Press, 1980). Copyright © 1980 by Rita Dove. Reprinted with permission of author.

DUHAMEL   "Snow White's Acne" (**42**) by Denise Duhamel, in *The Cortland Review* 11 (May 2000). Reprinted with permission of author.

ECCLES   "The Development of Children Ages 6 to 14" (**19**) by Jacquelynne S. Eccles, in *When School Is Out,* Vol. 9, No. 2, Fall 1999.

ECCLESIASTICUS   Ecclesiasticus 6:34-36 (**111**) and 37: 13-14 (**121**), New Revised Standard Version.

EDELMAN   "Reflections on Success" (**81, 110**) by Marian Wright Edelman, in *The Black Collegian Online: The Career Site for Students of Color*, www.black-collegian.com.

EDSON   "You" (**30**) in *The Wounded Breakfast* by Russell Edson. Copyright © 1985 by Russell Edson. Reprinted with permission of Wesleyan University Press, www.wesleyan.edu/wespress.

ELIOT   *Middlemarch* (**53**) by George Eliot, 1900.

ELKIND   *The Hurried Child: Growing Up Too Fast Too Soon* (7) by David Elkind, 1988.

EMERSON   *Journal*, December 1834 (55) by Ralph Waldo Emerson; *Journal*, November 1842 (105) by Ralph Waldo Emerson; "Self-Reliance" (145) in *Essays* by Ralph Waldo Emerson, 1841; and *Nature* (147) by Ralph Waldo Emerson, 1836.

EPSTEIN   "Moods (14 years old)" (76) by Sara Epstein, from www.literarymama.com. Reprinted with permission of author.

ERIKSON   *From Childhood and Society* (11) by Erik Erikson, 1950.

EZZO   Selection (18) by Gary Ezzo and Anne Marie Ezzo, on "Growing Families International," www.gfi.org.

FARMER   *What America Owes to Women* (83) by Lydia Hoyt Farmer, 1893.

FEARING   "Any Man's Advice to His Son" (102), in *Complete Poems* by Kenneth Fearing (National Poetry Foundation, 1997). Copyright © 1940 by Kenneth Fearing, renewed © 1968 by the Estate of Kenneth Fearing. Reprinted with permission of Russell & Volkening, Inc., as agents for the author.

FROMM   *The Art of Loving* (16) by Erich Fromm, 1956.

FROST   "The Road Not Taken" (120), in *Mountain Interval* by Robert Frost, 1920.

FULGHUM   *From Beginning to End: The Rituals of Our Lives* (10, 21) by Robert Fulghum, 1995.

GIBBONS   Reprinted with permission of John Gibbons (8).

GIBBONS   Reprinted with permission of Kendyl Gibbons (**99, 106, 119**).

GIBRAN   "On Self-Knowledge" (**3**), in *The Prophet* by Kahlil Gibran. Copyright 1923 by Kahlil Gibran and renewed 1951 by the Administrators C.T.A. of the Kahlil Gibran Estate and Mary G. Gibran. Reprinted with permission of Alfred A. Knopf, a division of Random House, Inc.

GIDE   *The Journals* (**151**) by André Gide, vol. 2, translated by Justin O'Brien, 1948.

GIEDD   Selection (**38**) by Jay Giedd, in "Beyond the Brain" by James Shreeve, in *National Geographic*, March 2005. "Frontline: Inside the Teenage Brain, Interview with Jay Giedd" (**54**), on PBS, www.pbs.org.

GILL   "Alterations" (**79**) by Wendy H. Gill, in *Literary Mama: A Magazine for the Maternally Inclined*, www.literarymama.com. Reprinted with permission of author.

HARRINGTON   "Life's Pilgrimage—Now and Forever" (**117**) by Donald S. Harrington. Reprinted with permission of Ilona H. Hancock.

HEBBLE   Reprinted with permission of Susan Morrison Hebble (**9, 33**).

HILBERRY   "Instruction" (**8**) by Conrad Hilberry, in *In the Heydays of His Eyes (taut jeans dancing): An Anthology of Poems about Being Young and Growing Up*, www.heydays.ws. Reprinted with permission of author.

HINE   *Rise and Fall of the American Teenager* (**49**) by Thomas Hine, 1999.

JAGGERS   "Passage" (**90**) by Trish Lindsey Jaggers, in *Literary Mama: A Magazine for the Maternally Inclined*, www.literarymama.com. Reprinted with permission of author.

JAMES   Selection (**30**) by William James, in *Field Guide to the American Teenager: A Parent's Companion* by Michael Riera and Joseph Di Prisco, 2000.

JARMAN   "Ground Swell" (**56**), in *Questions for Ecclesiastes* by Mark Jarman. Copyright © 1977 by Mark Jarman. All rights reserved. Reprinted with permission of author and Story Line Press.

JAWORSKI   "Rite of Passage" (**51**). Reprinted with permission of Birdie Jaworski.

KENNARD   "Boundary Man" (**86**) by Barbara Kennard, in *Literary Mama: A Magazine for the Maternally Inclined*, www.literarymama.com. Reprinted with permission of author.

KEYMAN   "Son of a Bitch" (**95**) by garrie keyman, in *Literary Mama: Reading for the Maternally Inclined,* edited by Andrea J. Buchanan and Amy Hudock (Emeryville, Calif.: Seal Press, 2006). Reprinted with permission of author.

KIDD   *The Secret Life of Bees* (**25**) by Sue Monk Kidd, 2003.

KINGSOLVER   *Animal Dreams* (**94**) by Barbara Kingsolver, 1990.

KIPLING   "If—" (**115**), in *Rewards and Fairies* by Rudyard Kipling, 1910.

KOLODNY   *How to Survive Your Adolescent's Adolescence* (**20**) by Robert C. Kolodny et al., 1984.

KUSHNER   *Living a Life that Matters: Resolving the Conflict between Conscience and Success* (**112**) by Harold S. Kushner, 2001.

LAWRENCE   "Virgin Youth" (**44**), in *Amores* by D. H. Lawrence, 1916.

LEADER   "Her Door" (**73**), in *Red Signature* by Mary Leader. Copyright © 1997 by Mary Leader. Reprinted with permission of Graywolf Press, Saint Paul, Minnesota.

LEVERTOV   "The Secret" (**149**), in *Poems 1960-1967* by Denise Levertov. Copyright © 1964 by Denise Levertov. Reprinted with permission of New Directions Publishing Corporation.

LINDSAY   "The Leaden-Eyed" (**147**), in *The Congo and Other Poems* by Vachel Lindsay, 1914.

LOCKLIN   "No Longer a Teenager" (**14**), in *The Life Force Poems* by Gerald I. Locklin (Water Row Press). Reprinted with permission of author.

LOEHR   "He: A Salvation Story for Man" (**39**), in *America, Fascism & God: Sermons from a Heretical Preacher*, 2005. Reprinted with permission of Davidson Loehr.

LORDE   "Hanging Fire" (**58**), in *The Collected Poems of Audre Lorde* by Audre Lorde. Copyright © 1978 by Audre Lorde. Reprinted with permission of W. W. Norton & Company, Inc.

LUX   "A Little Tooth" (**90**), in *The Drowned River: New Poems* by Thomas Lux. Copyright © 1990 by Thomas Lux. Reprinted with permission of Houghton Mifflin Company. All rights reserved.

MAGIE   *The Spring-time of Life; or, Advice to Youth* (**125**) by David Magie, 1855.

MASTEN   "Prepping the Children" (**52**). Reprinted with permission of Ric Masten.

MCKAY   "Adolescence" (**48**), in *Harlem Shadows* by Claude McKay, 1922.

MEYER   "Spiritual Growth Is for Everyone" (27). Reprinted with permission of Judith E. Meyer.

MICHENER   *The Fires of Spring* (110) by James Michener, 1949.

MILL   *On Liberty* (148) by John Stuart Mill, 1869.

MITCHELL   "Puppy Called Puberty" (41), in *Blue Coffee: Poems 1985-1996* by Adrian Mitchell (Northumberland: Bloodaxe Books, 1996). Copyright © 1996 by Adrian Mitchell. Reprinted with permission.

MURPHY   "Red" (45) by Karen Murphy, in *Moon Days: Creative Writings About Menstruation*, edited by Cassie Premo Steele, Ph.D, 1999. Reprinted with permission of Ash Tree Publishing.

NEMSER   "The Boy Was Young" (62), in *Moments of a Springtime* by Rudolph Nemser, 1967. Reprinted with permission of Rudolph Nemser's estate.

NEUFELD   Selection (74) by Gordon Neufeld, on "Making Sense of Kids," www.gordonneufeld.com. Reprinted with permission of author.

NIN   Selection (4) by Anaïs Nin, in *Girl in the Mirror: Mothers and Daughters in the Years of Adolescence* by Nancy L. Snyderman and Peg Streep, 2002.

OLMER   "On the Road to Womanhood" (138). Reprinted with permission of Ksenija Soster Olmer.

PATTON   "A World to Make" (107), "The Way" (113), and "True Teachers" (121), in *Services and Songs for the Celebration of Life* by Kenneth L. Patton, 1967. Reprinted with permission of Clarise E. Patton.

PEEBLES   "Coming of Sage" (122). Reprinted with permission of Linda Olson Peebles.

PERRIN   "Be as Frodo" (**117**), in *Goldenrods: Love Poetry for the Old &
Foolish* by Melinda Morris Perrin, 2005. Reprinted with permission of
author.

PIPHER   *Reviving Ophelia* (**7**) by Mary Pipher, 1994.

PITTMAN   Selection (**27**) by Frank Pittman, in *The Columbia World of
Quotations*, edited by Robert Andrews, Mary Biggs, and Michael Seidel
et al., 1996.

POE   "In Youth I Have Known One" (**131**), in *Tamerlane and Other
Poems* by Edgar Allan Poe, 1827.

PROVERBS   Proverbs 3:1 (**95**), New Living Translation. Proverbs 4:20-27
(**107**) and Proverbs 3:13-18 (**115**), New Revised Standard Version.

PRUITT   *Your Adolescent: Emotional, Behavioral, and Cognitive Development from Early Adolescence through the Teen Years* (**12**, **38**), edited by
David B. Pruitt, 1999.

QUINDLEN   "Parental Rites" (**36**), in *Thinking Out Loud: On the Personal, the Political, the Public and the Private* by Anna Quindlen, 1994.

RAMSEY   "Hand-Shadows" (**100**), in *Hand-Shadows* by Jarold Ramsey
(New York: Quarterly Review of Literature, 1989). Copyright © 1989 by
Jarold Ramsey. Reprinted with permission of author.

RITTENBERG   "Tomorrow Will Be a Better Day" (**152**) by Josh Rittenberg, from *This I Believe* (NPR, February 27, 2006). Copyright © 2006
by. Reprinted with permission of Henry Holt and Company, LLC.

ROOSEVELT   Selection (**152**) by Franklin D. Roosevelt, in *Great Quotes
for Great Educators*, edited by Todd Whitaker, 2005.

SAFFORD   "Map of the Journey in Progress" (**104**), in *Walking Toward Morning* by Victoria Safford, 2003. Reprinted with permission of author.

SALINGER   *The Catcher in the Rye* (**33**) by J. D. Salinger, 1951.

SAMS   *The Whisper of the River* (**46**) by Ferrol Sams, 1986. Copyright © 1984 by Ferrol Sams. Reprinted with permission of Peachtree Publishers.

SARTON   "Now I Become Myself" (**123**), in *Collected Poems 1930-1993* by May Sarton. Copyright © 1993, 1988, 1984, 1980, 1974 by May Sarton. Reprinted with permission of W. W. Norton & Company, Inc.

SCHWEITZER   *Memoirs of Childhood and Youth* (**146**) by Albert Schweitzer, 1924.

SEARL   "Passage" (**28**) by Edward Searl.

SEARS   "When The Big Blue Light Comes a Whirling Up Behind" (**131**), in *I Want to Be a Crowd: Poems and Commentary* by Peter Sears, 1978. Reprinted with permission of author.

SEXTON   "Little Girl, My String Bean, My Lovely Woman" (**67**), in *Live or Die* by Anne Sexton. Copyright © 1966 by Anne Sexton, renewed 1994 by Linda G. Sexton. Reprinted with permission of Houghton Mifflin Company. All rights reserved.

SHAKESPEARE   *A Winter's Tale* (**49**) by William Shakespeare, 1623.

SHAPIRO   "Poet" (**55**), in *New and Selected Poems 1940-1986* by Karl Shapiro (Chicago: The University of Chicago Press, 1987). Copyright © 1987 by Karl Shapiro. Reprinted with permission of Wieser & Elwell, Inc.

SILKO   *Ceremony* (**27**) by Leslie Marmon Silko, 1977.

SOSTER-OLMER   "On the Road to Womanhood" (**138**) by Ksenija Soster-Olmer, in "Moon Rising: The Making of a Menarche Ritual," in *Mothering* 109 (November/December 2001), as found at www.mothering.com/community_tools/teen_voices/first-moon.html.

SPENCER   "The Discovery of Sex" (**139**), in *Pomegranate* by Debra Spencer. Copyright © 2004 by Debra Spencer. Reprinted with permission of Hummingbird Press.

STAFFORD   "Fifteen" (**143**), in *The Way It Is: New and Selected Poems* by William Stafford. Copyright © 1966, 1998 by the estate of William Stafford. Reprinted with permission of Graywolf Press, Saint Paul, Minnesota.

STEINBERG AND LEVINE   *You and Your Adolescent* (**55**) by Laurence Steinberg and Ann Levine, 1990.

STEINEM   "If Men Could Menstruate" (**42**), in *Outrageous Acts and Everyday Rebellions* by Gloria Steinem, 1983.

STOTT   *Documentary Expression and Thirties America* (**15**) by William Stott, 1973.

TAYLOR   "Biting Our Tongues" (**76**). Reprinted with permission of Alan C. Taylor.

TEASDALE   "Wisdom" (**125**) by Sara Teasdale, 1917.

THOREAU   *Walden* (**144**, **151**) by Henry David Thoreau, 1854.

VIORST   "Did I Do Something Wrong?" (**85**), in *Suddenly Sixty and Other Shocks of Later Life* by Judith Viorst, 2000. Published by Simon & Schuster. Text copyright © 2000 by Judith Viorst. Reprinted with permission of Lescher & Lescher, Ltd. All rights reserved.

WELLS   "The Spiritual Journey Home" (**29**). Reprinted with permission of Hannah Wells.

WESTON   Selection (**135**) by Robert T. Weston, in *Cup of Strength: Readings in Time of Sorrow and Bereavement*, edited by Robert T. Weston. Reprinted with permission of Richard Weston-Jones.

WHICKER   "Pushing 7 ½, Falling Into 8" (**34**) and "Caught Before Flight" (**135**) by Vicki Whicker, in *Twelve Los Angeles Poets* (Los Angeles: Bombshelter Press, 2002). Copyright © 2002 by Vicki Whicker. Reprinted with permission of author.

WHITE   "Youth and Age" (**114**), in *Poems and Sketches of E. B. White* by E. B. White. Copyright © 1981 by E. B. White. Reprinted with permission of HarperCollins Publishers.

WHITMAN   "Preface" (**103**), "Carol of Occupations" (**112**), and "I Sing the Body Electric" (**134, 142**), in *Leaves of Grass* by Walt Whitman, 1855.

WOLFE   *Look Homeward, Angel* (**99**) by Thomas Wolfe, 1929.

WOLPE   "As My Daughter Bleeds, So Do I" (**82**) by Valerie Root Wolpe. Copyright © 2000. Reprinted with permission of author.

WOODS-MURPHY   "Candles for My Daughter" (**4**) by Maryann Woods-Murphy, in *UUWorld* XVI: 4 (July/August 2002). Reprinted with permission of author.

WOOLF   "Hours in a Library" (**7**) by Virginia Woolf, in *Times Literary Supplement*, November 30, 1916.

WUTHNOW   *Growing Up Religious: Christians and Jews and Their Journeys of Faith* (**17**) by Robert Wuthnow, 1999.